I0100545

The Army and Ideology in Indonesia

This book is an analysis of Indonesia's civil-military relations in the post-1998 reform era. It focuses on the political thinking of the Indonesian Army during the time of democratic consolidation.

The book examines the army (Tentara Nasional Indonesia Angkatan Darat: TNI AD), a pivotal player in the political scene of Indonesian state, and the aspect of military ideology development. Based on in-depth interviews with civilian and military figures and applying process tracing methodology and empirical analysis surrounding the appearance of military thinking, the book argues that the Indonesian military pursues to sustain its political power by propagating a set of values construed as moral compass for all members of society. Specifically, the book discusses the origins and impacts of 'proxy war' and *bela negara* ('defend the state'), which was promoted by former TNI Commander Gatot Nurmantyo (2015–2017) and former Defence Minister Ryamizard Ryacudu (2014–2019), respectively. The authors demonstrate that both ideologies facilitate expansion of the military's influence in all aspects of life and protection of its corporate interests in the age of democracy.

Offering insights for theoretical discussion on the influence of military ideology to civil-military relations, particularly in the post-authoritarian period, this book will be of interest to academics and policy makers in the fields of Southeast Asian politics, Asian politics, and civil-military relations.

Muhamad Haripin is Researcher at the Centre for Political Studies–Indonesian Institute of Sciences (Pusat Penelitian Politik–LIPI), Jakarta. He is also the author of *Civil–Military Relations in Indonesia: The Politics of Military Operations Other Than War* (Routledge, 2019).

Adhi Priamarizki is Visiting Fellow at S. Rajaratnam School of International Studies, Nanyang Technological University, Singapore.

Keoni Indrabayu Marzuki is Associate Research Fellow at S. Rajaratnam School of International Studies, Nanyang Technological University, Singapore.

Routledge Contemporary Southeast Asia Series

The aim of this series is to publish original, high-quality work by both new and established scholars on all aspects of Southeast Asia.

Ethnographies of Development and Globalization in the Philippines
Emergent Socialities and the Governing of Precarity
Edited by Koki Seki

The Political Economy of Growth in Vietnam
Between States and Markets
Guanie Lim

ASEAN and Power in International Relations
ASEAN, the EU, and the Contestation of Human Rights
Jamie D. Stacey

The Army and Ideology in Indonesia
From *Dwifungsi* to *Bela Negara*
Muhamad Haripin, Adhi Priamarizki, and Keoni Indrabayu Marzuki

The 2018 and 2019 Indonesian Elections
Identity Politics and Regional Perspectives
Edited by Leonard C Sebastian and Alexander R Arifianto

Embodied Performativity in Southeast Asia
Multidisciplinary Corporealities
Edited by Stephanie Burridge

For more information about this series, please visit: www.routledge.com/ Routledge-Contemporary-Southeast-Asia-Series/book-series/RCSEA

The Army and Ideology in Indonesia

From *Dwifungsi* to *Bela Negara*

Muhamad Haripin, Adhi Priamarizki, and Keoni Indrabayu Marzuki

Routledge
Taylor & Francis Group

LONDON AND NEW YORK

First published 2021
by Routledge
2 Park Square, Milton Park, Abingdon, Oxon OX14 4RN

and by Routledge
52 Vanderbilt Avenue, New York, NY 10017

Routledge is an imprint of the Taylor & Francis Group, an informa business

British Library Cataloguing-in-Publication Data
A catalogue record for this book is available from the British Library

Library of Congress Cataloging-in-Publication Data
Names: Haripin, Muhamad, author. | Adhi Priamarizki, author. | Marzuki,
    Keoni Indrabayu, author.
Title: The army and ideology in Indonesia : from dwifungsi to bela
    negara / Muhamad Haripin, Adhi Priamarizki, and Keoni Indrabayu
    Marzuki.
Description: Abingdon, Oxon ; New York, NY : Routledge, 2021. |
    Includes bibliographical references and index.
Identifiers: LCCN 2020022202 | ISBN 9780367553050 (hardback) |
    ISBN 9781003092926 (ebook)
Subjects: LCSH: Civil-military relations—Political aspects—Indonesia. |
    Indonesia—Armed Forces—Political activity. | Indonesia—Politics and
    government—1998–
Classification: LCC JQ766.C58 H37 2010 | DDC 322/.509598—dc23
LC record available at https://lccn.loc.gov/2020022202

ISBN: 978-0-367-55305-0 (hbk)
ISBN: 978-0-367-55308-1 (pbk)
ISBN: 978-1-003-09292-6 (ebk)

Typeset in Times New Roman
by Apex CoVantage, LLC

For

Mutiara Arumsari
M.H.

Shinta Andriani
A.P.

Ni Luh Putu Ayumi Yuttari Putri
K.I.M

Contents

Illustrations

Tables

Figures

Abbreviations

ABRI	Angkatan Bersenjata Republik Indonesia, Indonesian military and police institution in pre-democratisation period
ASEAN	Association of Southeast Asian Nations
BKR	Badan Keamanan Rakyat, People's Security Body
FPI	Front Pembela Islam, Islamic Defender Front
GAM	Gerakan Aceh Merdeka, Free Aceh Movement
Golkar	Golongan Karya, Functional Group
Ipoleksosbudhankam	*Ideologi, politik, ekonomi, sosial, budaya, pertahanan, dan keamanan* – ideology, politics, economy, social, culture, defence, and security
ISIS	Islamic State of Iraq and Syria
KGB	*Komunisme Gaya Baru*, new style of communism
KNIL	Koninklijk Nederlands Indisch Leger, Royal Netherlands East Indies Army
Kostrad	Komando Cadangan Strategis TNI Angkatan Darat, Army Strategic Reserve Command
Koter	Komando teritorial, territorial command
KSAD	Kepala Staf TNI Angkatan Darat, Army Chief of Staff
Lemhanas	Lembaga Ketahanan Nasional, National Resilience Institute
LGBT	Lesbian, gay, bisexual, and transgender
Nasakom	*Nasionalis, agama, komunis* or nationalism, religion, communism
NGO	Non-governmental organisation
NKRI	Negara Kesatuan Republik Indonesia, Unitary State of the Republic of Indonesia
PDI-P	Partai Demokrasi Indonesia Perjuangan, Indonesian Democratic Party of Struggle

PETA	Pembela Tanah Air, Defender of the Homeland; Japanese–trained militias during the Japanese occupation in Indonesia, in the 1940s
PKS	Partai Keadilan Sejahtera, Prosperity and Justice Party
Polri	Kepolisian Negara Republik Indonesia, Indonesian National Police
TKR	Tentara Keamanan Rakyat, People's Security Army
TNI	Tentara Nasional Indonesia, Indonesian National Armed Forces
TNI AD	Tentara Nasional Indonesia Angkatan Darat, Indonesian Army
TNI AL	Tentara Nasional Indonesia Angkatan Laut, Indonesian Navy
TNI AU	Tentara Nasional Indonesia Angkatan Udara, Indonesian Air Force
Wantannas	Dewan Ketahanan Nasional, National Resilience Council

Acknowledgements

We would like to thank our colleagues and researchers at the Centre for Political Studies–Indonesian Institute of Sciences (Pusat Penelitian Politik–LIPI) and S. Rajaratnam School of International Studies, Nanyang Technological University (RSIS NTU), who had been tremendously supporting the conduct of this study.

We also wish to express our gratitude to our informants, who consist of not only active and retired officers from the Indonesian National Armed Forces (Tentara Nasional Indonesia: TNI) but also civilians in various ministerial offices as well as non-governmental organisations. Their insights and stories have greatly shaped our understanding about the role of ideology on Indonesian military politics.

Last but not least, we thank anonymous reviewers, Dorothea Schaefter, and Alexandra de Brauw from Routledge for their constructive suggestions and enthusiasm in publishing this project.

Muhamad Haripin, Adhi Priamarizki, and Keoni Marzuki
Jakarta and Singapore, June 2020

1 Introduction

The army and ideology in Indonesia

Muhamad Haripin, Adhi Priamarizki, and Keoni Indrabayu Marzuki

The Indonesian Army (Tentara Nasional Indonesia Angkatan Darat: TNI AD) has been a dominant force, both within the military organisation and in the national politics of Indonesia. The army has a tutelary belief as the guardian of the Indonesian nation – a belief that is rooted in the armed forces' experiences during the early days of the founding of the republic. The army was self-established, organised, and armed organically following the surrender of Japan imperial government and the proclamation of Indonesian independence on August 17, 1945.[1] Further underlying the belief is their experiences in guerrilla resistance against the Dutch's attempt to regain control of Indonesia during 1945–1949, which earned the soldiers a role to play in policy formulation as well as to shape the national political life. In justifying this belief, the army formulated doctrines that accommodate their interests and presence in politics.

The Indonesian Army also held deep-seated distrust of civilian elites and saw them as weak, incapable, and disorganised groups – a view that became prevalent and deeply embedded within the military following Sukarno's, the first Indonesian president, refusal to support General Sudirman's, the first commander of Indonesian military, guerrilla resistance against the Dutch following the breakdown of the Renville Agreement in 1948.[2] Various experiences following this consequential turning point led to deep embeddedness of the military in all aspects of life, later the army as the backbone of the authoritarian regime of New Order (Orde Baru) from 1966 until 1998 under President Suharto, the successor of Sukarno. Political economy change in the late 1990s, however, brought democratisation and compelled the Indonesian military to undertake a reform.

Previous studies on the ideology of Indonesian army particularly during the New Order era argue that the dynamics of internal thinking among officers have been a result of collective self-examination on the potential and imminent external challenges encountered by the state and how the military has been or will be affected by them. In this sense, however, we must be aware that 'external challenges' believed by the army elites, for instance the threats of foreign invasion and territorial infringements, do not always mean entirely out of the realm of military. Instead, such assessment often reflects intra-division and infightings among the high-level officers.[3] In contrast with popular belief that the military is a cohesive institution and bounded by organisational discipline, the very existence of dynamics of internal debate itself suggests otherwise. The 'external challenges' discourses were brought in by particularly one faction to justify the institutional necessity to adapt with new political circumstances; meanwhile others might suggest different outlook or even demand no change at all. This army factionalism was argued to be part of cut-throat competition among military elites to obtain President Suharto's favour. Different camps wanted to win the president's political support and business channels.

In this regard, we see an established pattern of political competition – at least – between two major camps throughout the history of Suharto's New Order: ideology has often been exploited by the competing parties to justify their political stance in front of dictator ruler and to gain economic privileges. We will elaborate this discussion in the succeeding sections.

This study argues that the introduction of 'proxy war' and *bela negara* (herein after 'defend the state') – twin ideologies under the duumvirates of Indonesian National Armed Forces (Tentara Nasional Indonesia: TNI) Commander General Gatot Nurmantyo (2015–2017) and Defence Minister Ryamizard Ryacudu (2014–2019) – demonstrates a new pattern of army's ideological trend in Indonesia's democratisation period. 'Proxy war' narrative gained nationwide recognition following Gatot's ascension to national political scene in July 2014. Susilo Bambang Yudhoyono, the sixth president of the Republic of Indonesia, appointed him as the army chief of staff, replacing General Budiman. In many of his public statements, Gatot often reiterated the danger of 'proxy war' in Indonesia. Following the tradition of all-encompassing concept of threats in army establishment, he explained that many countries and non-state actors have great interests of Indonesia's wealth and natural resources and will do whatever they can to exert influence and domination over the archipelago. The instrument of proxy war, according to Gatot, is non-military, and the subterfuge nature of the instrument caused identifying the actors a difficult undertaking. Yet, Gatot asserted that the result of their insidious works can be seen from the various excesses of unbridled liberal democracy (*demokrasi kebablasan*) that has been instituted since *Reformasi* in 1998, including economic overdependence, the domination of foreign companies in national oil and gas sector, as well as cultural appropriation by other countries. This foreign infiltration is then called a 'proxy war,' borrowing the term from Cold War period when the United States of America and the Soviet Union competed for world domination through war and other means via proxy beyond their own national territory.

Gatot's proxy war gained further popularity after he was appointed as TNI commander in July 2015, replacing General Moeldoko. The newly appointed military commander conducted a series of public lectures in universities and private institutions on the topic of patriotism and the danger of 'proxy war.' In his lectures and speeches, for instance, Gatot frequently emphasised the crisis of drug abuse among Indonesian youths as a result of foreign infiltration. On top of personal promotion of 'proxy war,' there was a strong indication that he took advantage of his position as the highest-ranking officer in the military to promote the ideology, as evident from the promotion of the concept by various branches of the TNI at different level of the chain of command.[4]

Meanwhile, Defence Minister Ryamizard Ryacudu, also a former army chief of staff, promoted the ideology of *bela negara* ('defend the state').[5] Ryamizard was not the first state official who systematically explained the logics behind *bela negara*, as the concept has gained prominence since as early as Susilo Bambang Yudhoyono's presidency (2004–2009 and 2009–2014). However, Ryamizard is arguably the most prominent proponent behind the nationwide promotion of this initiative, which reflects the latest government campaign to instil patriotism, nationalism, and the state ideology of Pancasila among citizens. *Bela negara* aims to provide some degree of basic paramilitary training and civics education programme for civilians. Taken within this context, the concept of nationalism and/or patriotism that *bela negara* aims to instil is not regular patriotism but rather a distinctively militaristic interpretation of the word. Subsequently, it includes not only standard curriculum on official national history and its adaptation to modern context but also a vehement apprehension towards ideas and concepts that are foreign and perceived to be harmful to Indonesia's way of life. Ryamizard frequently invoked caution, perhaps exaggeratingly, against the dangers of LGBT (lesbian, gay, bisexual, and transgender) community, to which the solution would be participating in *bela negara* training. To advance this initiative, Ryamizard leveraged on his ministerial position to forge cooperation with other ministries and public institutions, including schools and state-owned enterprises, as well as private institutions to conduct training and seminar related with *bela negara*. The initiative is undoubtedly an ambitious one, as Ryamizard aims to recruit 100 million *bela negara* cadres by 2025. This move invited uproar among civil society due to concern that it would militarise civilian polity and open a path for the establishment of state-sponsored militia.

Based on these sketches, this study will address the following questions: why does the army establishment promulgate military-based ideology in a 'stable' and 'democratic' political environment – to date, democratisation has been underway for 20 years in Indonesia, and five consecutive national elections, not to mention regional elections since 2005, have been held peacefully? What does it tell us about the army's political contemporary outlook? This research argues that, in contrast with previous army's ideologies, the 'proxy war' and 'defend the state' (*bela negara*) have demonstrated a rather peculiar trend in contrast with the tradition of Indonesian army political thinking. If military ideology has proliferated as a defence mechanism against extra-military intervention in the past, the concepts of 'proxy war' and *bela negara* have been more aggressive in nature – in the sense that both ideologies are inherently geared to ensconce the military's influence in all aspects of life.

Classic civil-military relations literatures have pointed out attempts of military intervention using 'the guardian of the nation' claim and doctrine as foundation to legitimise its action.[6] The arrival of democratisation in Indonesia supposedly calls the military to come up with a new doctrine which fits with the new democratic setting. The case of Gatot's 'proxy war' and Ryamizard's *bela negara* shows that encroachment to political realm can be facilitated without officially altering military ideology. In other words, the existence of a military ideology that fits with democratic idea provides no guarantee to keep the armed forces in the barrack. Creation of ancillary thinking, such as Gatot's 'proxy war' and Ryamizard's *bela negara*, surfaced as a form of adaptation towards democratic environment and reform pressure, a defence mechanism to protect military corporate interests. This will be the theoretical contribution of this book.

To elaborate the main argument, the structure of discussion will be given as follows. First, we discuss the historical development of army ideology from the 1940s to New Order era. This period is crucial as formative years of *tentara rakyat* (people's army) identity and *dwifungsi* (dual-function) doctrine. The second part of the discussion will elaborate on how the Indonesian army adapts from the authoritarian New Order era to democracy started out in 1998. During this period, the old but highly effective *NKRI harga mati* concept (figuratively meaning the Unitary State of the Republic of Indonesia is everything; 'we should defend the country at all costs') gained prominence. It served two purposes; first, to consolidate internal military and second, to undermine reform pressure and external critics against the defence establishment. The ideology came at a very interesting moment when the country was at the critical juncture of democratic transition. The army was at the receiving end of political attacks for its past abuse of power and human rights misconducts in conflict areas such as Aceh and Papua. Civilian politician and non-governmental organisations formed a ring of fire to delimit military role and function. However, as will be discussed later, *NKRI harga mati* has proven to be an effective discursive weapon to neutralise the opposition against the army's political power.

Third, the army ideology expands with the promulgation of 'proxy war' and *bela negara* in the presidency of Joko Widodo, a civilian politician with little political experience in national level. Widodo's rise to power in 2014 has shocked not only conventional political gameplay in Jakarta but also the military in general – particularly because Widodo floated the *poros maritim dunia* ('global maritime fulcrum'), implying priority of the navy and air forces, possibly at the expense of the army. Nonetheless, even since his first days in offices, the internal political dynamics has compelled Widodo to bolster his political standings by aligning with the army to offset his minimal political support. He appointed an army general, Gatot Nurmantyo, as TNI commander – a break in the tradition where the position of TNI commander is rotated between the three services. Furthermore, Widodo shows little hesitation to support the army's expanding agenda on non-defence affairs. Indeed, this is a defining moment for his presidency that, this study argues, defines the pattern of contemporary civil-military relations and in turn becomes an enabling environment for the proliferation of new army ideologies: 'proxy war' and *bela negara*.

Prior to examining the main topics, we would like to discuss the existing scholarships on civil-military relations in post-authoritarian Indonesia and to locate our study within the discipline. Afterwards, we will explain the conceptual framework utilised in analysing the political as well as historical trajectory of Indonesian army's political thinking.

Previous studies

The fall of the Suharto regime in 1998 not only brought about a number of changes in Indonesia political system, such as the introduction of direct elections, a full-fledged multiparty system, presidential term limits, decentralisation, and direct regional election, but also started military reform in the country. The Indonesian military was seen as part of the regime as the New Order deployed armed troops as its repressive tool to silence oppositions and thus was considered to be one of the critical elements that needed to be reformed. Since the country's independence, the Indonesian armed forces rejected a strategic outlook that limit their roles only in defence realm, which is based on the justification that the military should play a significant role in state building.[7] The mounted pressures for reform forced the Indonesian military to accept democratic demands and self-initiated the process of military reform. In responding to those demands, the internal power struggle within the military became the primary factor. Factions within the Indonesian armed forces took different approaches to show their ascendancy, which in the end produced a mixed response to the growing democratic demands.[8]

Although democratic pressures managed to extract the military from formal politics and strip the Indonesian armed forces of its privilege as a socio-political force, it did not entirely ransack TNI's privileges.[9] Ambiguous definition of some TNI's roles, the persistence of the army's sprawling territorial command structure, military business activities, and military impunity are some of the issues that the military reform failed to address.[10] Tug of war in the form of negotiation and bargain between reformers and the old guard within the military, between political and military elites, and between civil society and the state nuanced the process of Indonesia's military reform.[11] For example, the Susilo Bambang Yudhoyono administration attempted to strengthen military professionalism and its accountability to the state by limiting the military formal business activities. But this endeavour failed to curb the armed forces' informal military business activities.[12] Nevertheless, the increments of the defence budget helped the military to reduce its dependency to off-budget funding, which previously amounted to about 70 per cent of TNI's budget.[13] This example reflects Yudhoyono's accommodative approach towards the military – by not pushing for radical reforms but at the same time employing other measures to make the military more accountable to the state.[14]

Like his predecessor, President Joko Widodo also seems to implement a similar approach when it comes to dealing with the military. In the broader scheme of things, Widodo's accommodative approach means that the trend of civil-military relations in the post-Suharto era largely remained in status quo with continued evolution of the military's role as it adjusts to a new political realm.[15] Despite this relatively constant trends, recent developments triggered some questions towards the trajectory of civil-military relations in Indonesia. General Gatot Nurmantyo and Defence Minister Ryamizard Ryacudu came up with the idea and notion of 'proxy war' and *bela negara* to highlight potential security threats to the country, and thereby requiring the military's role to counteract them. At face value, their bold statements and claims hinted the military's intention to keep its vague position in handling security threats, which may entail some degree of political involvement, despite the civilian government's success in stabilising political and economic condition following the downfall of Suharto.

As seen previously, most studies on Indonesian military focus on the involvement of the armed forces in politics rather than solely emphasising on their ideological development. Peter Britton argued that Javanese knighthood principle heavily shaped the Indonesian military thinking. Moreover, Britton noted that the principle refuses clear distinction between civilian and military duties.[16] A study from Leonard C. Sebastian explored the ideology behind Indonesia's use of military force.[17] Sebastian's study showed that TNI adopts a pragmatic approach of military ideology, which is driven by the objective to put national security above all. Furthermore, the military elites largely monopolised the definition of national security. Thus, as long as those elites reject democratisation idea, there will be always a possibility of an unstable civil-military relations. Furthermore, the inability of civilian institutions to deliver good performance could be another reason for the military to intervene.[18]

Stable domestic political environment ushered in by the democratic consolidation era supposedly downplays the use of realpolitik ideology of the TNI, as democratisation values have been infused into the military through various measures, such as dropping social politics course in the cadet school curriculum. In addition, democratisation supposedly pervades the military with democratic ideals and norms, including civilian supremacy, which calls for military subordination to civilian authority. Despite the winding and arduous process of military reform, the current circumstance has shown a rather contrasting fact – that the Indonesian military seemed to subscribe and espouse ideas that suggest an aspiration to enhance its presence in politics. Against this backdrop, our research aims to analyse this military resistance against democratic reform that is reflected from the proliferation of 'proxy war' and *bela negara* ideologies by General Gatot Nurmantyo and Minister of Defence Ryamizard Ryacudu.

Conceptual framework: military ideology and intervention

It would be almost impossible to find a military that is completely apolitical, as state needs the armed forces' constant support to ensure state's stability.[19] Military intervention in politics has a wide spectrum, and its manifestation varies from influencing policy and decision-making process at one end of the extreme to launching coup d'état and establishing its own government on the other end. To minimise the discourse debate, this study employs Samuel Finer's definition on military intervention[20]:

> The armed forces' constrained substitution of their own policies and/ or their persons, for those of the recognised civilian authorities. The military may pursue such intervention by acts of commission but also by acts of omission. It may act against the wishes of its government; or it may refuse to act when called on by its government.

Eric A. Nordlinger labelled interventionist officers as praetorian soldiers. The term 'praetorianism' can be traced back to the Praetorian Guards of the

Roman Empire, which was famous for their interventionist behaviour, ranging from overthrowing emperors to rigging senate's election of successive emperors. According to Nordlinger, praetorianism is "a situation in which military officers are major or pre-dominant political actors by virtue of their actual or threatened use of force."[21] Praetorian military tends to intervene in daily politics and even dominate the executive, which are not necessarily relevant to its actual duties.[22]

The military legitimates this praetorian behaviour by self-proclaiming itself as 'the guardian' or 'the saviour' of the nation to establish political leverage and subsequently expands their role to encompass aspects beyond the traditional defence affairs.[23] Ideology turns into an essential foundation in facilitating the expansion. The military requires a justification to shroud the motive with a noble robe. The legacy of military's formative experience, particularly those who went through revolutionary struggle, moulded the self-determination of being the sole protector of the country.[24]

While intervention due to the failure to meet the demand or interest of military officers occurred in some cases,[25] interventionist ideology made encroachment to political realm possible without being preceded by any catastrophic political instability and extremely severe economic downturn. Alfred Stepan's seminal works on Latin American militaries noted what he called as 'new professionalism,' of which military expansion beyond defence affairs is tolerated in order to address a wide range of threats. Stepan also emphasised that this 'new professionalism' is embedded in the national security ideology and doctrine.[26]

A study from Kees Koonings and Dirk Kruijt on political armies echoed Stepan's point, arguing that ideologies and doctrines act as a crucial transmitter of political orientation of the military into more specific guidelines for political intervention or direct rule.[27] Here we see that military ideology enables the armed forces' expansion beyond the defence realm. Nonetheless, democratisation generated a different circumstance for military and even forced certain ideological change in order to reform the armed forces.

The emergence of democratisation forced military to limit their involvement in politics and channel its aspirations via constitutional ways. Alagappa underlined the influence of democratic transition in the military's withdrawal from politics.[28] The military's commitment to democratic rule as well as its obedience to democratically elected political elites is paramount for consolidating democracy.[29] Democratisation demands the military to be subordinated under the supervision and oversight of civilian government, which are essential to form effective civilian control. In post-authoritarian setting, strengthening civilian control and professionalising the military are generally two main objectives that are critical to achieve a new equilibrium of a stable civil-military relation.

Based on this background, the democratic setting supposedly abolished the interventionist thinking of military and stimulated a formulation of an ideology that fits under the framework of democracy. Post-authoritarian Indonesian military, however, showcased a peculiar symptom that contradicted the earlier discussion. Following the fall of the New Order regime, TNI embarked on its reform journey, notably withdrawing from politics and abolishing interventionist doctrine. The most recent development, however, displayed an intriguing case. The introduction of *bela negara* and 'proxy war,' as promoted by the TNI Commander General Gatot Nurmantyo (2015–2017) and Defence Minister Ryamizard Ryacudu (2014–2019), further encapsulated the intention to preserve political influence of TNI. Therefore, the case of TNI after the 1998 *Reformasi* suggests that the absence of an interventionist ideology did not prevent the encroachment to politics. We will elaborate the puzzle further in the following chapters.

Notes

1 Salim Said, "The Political Role of the Indonesian Military: Past, Present and Future," *Asian Journal of Social Science* 15, 1 (1987): p. 16.
2 Renvile Agreement was one of the negotiations between the governments of Indonesia and the Netherlands during the revolutionary war period, 1945–1949. The agreement caused Indonesia to lose control of the current West Java province and most parts of Central Java, which undermined the legitimacy of Indonesian government at that time.
3 We can see the internal competing interests when the army encountered strong democratic pressure during the late Suharto years. Some of the pivotal issues that divided the officers were the extent of military's political roles and human rights accountability. See particularly Chapter 5 of Jun Honna, *Military Politics and Democratization in Indonesia* (London: Routledge, 2003).
4 For example, see Gede Moenanto, "Wawasan Kebangsaan dan Bela Negara di Tengah Arus Proxy War," *Tribunnews.com*, May 30, 2016, www.tribunnews.com/metropolitan/2016/05/30/wawasan-kebangsaan-dan-bela-negara-di-tengah-arus-proxy-war, accessed 28 June 2019; Evie AD, "Danlantamal II Adakan Komsos TNI Matra Laut TA 2018 di TPI Muara Angke," *Radio Republik Indonesia*, March 30, 2018, http://rri.co.id/post/berita/508537/press_release/danlantamal_iii_adakan_komsos_tni_matra_laut_ta_2018_di_tpi_muara_angke.html, accessed June 28, 2019; and Tentara Nasional Indonesia Angkatan Udara, "Mewaspadai Proxy War, Lanud Iswahjudi Adakan Komsos TNI," September 15, 2017, https://tni-au.mil.id/mewaspadai-proxy-war-lanud-iwj-adakan-komsos-tni-2/, accessed June 28, 2019.
5 Other publications have translated *bela negara* differently. Rather than literal translation of 'defend the state,' which is used in this study, they chose to contextualise the concept as 'state defence' or 'defend the nation.' See, for instance, Bhatara Ibnu Reza, "The Dangerous Ideology Behind Bela Negara," *New Mandala*, January 25, 2017, www.newmandala.org/dangerous-ideology-behind-bela-negara/, accessed May 16, 2017; Bhatara Ibnu Reza, "Bela Negara: Thinly Veiled Militarisation of the Civilian Population," *Indonesia at Melbourne*,

July 12, 2016, http://indonesiaatmelbourne.unimelb.edu.au/bela-negara-thinly-veiled-militarisation-of-the-civilian-population/, accessed May 16, 2017; and Institute for Policy Analysis of Conflict, *Update on the Indonesian Military's Influence* (Jakarta: Institute for Policy Analysis of Conflict, 2016), pp. 11–12.

6 Amos Perlmutter, *The Military and Politics in Modern Times* (New Haven and London: Yale University Press, 1977); Eric A. Nordlinger, *Soldiers in Politics: Military Coups and Governments* (Englewood Cliffs, NJ: Prentice-Hall, 1977); Kees Koonings and Dirk Kruijt, "Epilogue: Political Armies Between Continuity and Demise," in *Political Armies: The Military and Nation Building in the Age of Democracy*, eds. Kees Koonings and Dirk Kruijt (New Yorks: Zed Books, 2002), pp. 333–347; Aqil Shah, *The Army and Democracy: Military Politics in Pakistan* (Cambridge, MA: Harvard University Press, 2014).

7 Leonard C. Sebastian, *Realpolitik Ideology: Indonesia's Use of Military Force* (Singapore: ISEAS, 2006), p. 323.

8 Jun Honna, *Military Politics and Democratization in Indonesia* (London: Routledge, 2003), p. 3.

9 Marcus Mietzner, *Military Politics, Islam, and the State in Indonesia: From Turbulent Transition to Democratic Consolidation* (Singapore: ISEAS, 2009), p. 361.

10 Harold Crouch, *Political Reform in Indonesia After Soeharto* (Singapore: ISEAS, 2010), pp. 153–174.

11 Jun Honna, "Security Challenges and Military Reform in Post-authoritarian Indonesia: The Impact of Separatism, Terrorism, and Communal Violence," in *The Politics of Military Reform: Experiences From Indonesia and Nigeria*, eds. Jürgen Rüland, Maria-Gabriela Manea, and Hans Born (Heidelberg: Springer, 2013), p. 196.

12 A study finds three forms of the Indonesian military's entrepreneurial endeavours, namely, formal business, informal business, and criminal economy. See Danang Widoyoko, et al., *Bisnis Militer Mencari Legitimasi* (Jakarta: ICW, 2003), pp. 12–13.

13 Marcus Mietzner, "The Political Marginalization of the Military in Indonesia," in *The Political Resurgence of the Military in Southeast Asia*, ed. Marcus Mietzner (London and New York: Routledge, 2011), p. 135.

14 Leonard C. Sebastian and Iis Gindarsah, "Taking Stock of Military Reform in Indonesia," in *The Politics of Military Reform: Experiences From Indonesia and Nigeria*, eds. Jürgen Rüland, Maria-Gabriela Manea, and Hans Born (Heidelberg: Springer, 2013), p. 54.

15 Evan A. Laksmana, "Indonesia's Modernizing Military: Suharto's New Order Is Old News," *Foreign Affairs*, September 3, 2015.

16 See Peter A. Britton, *Profesionalisme dan Ideologi Militer Indonesia: Perspektif Tradisi-Tradisi Jawa dan Barat* (Jakarta: LP3ES, 1996).

17 Sebastian, *Realpolitik Ideology*.

18 Ibid.

19 Zoltan Barany, *The Soldier and the Changing State: Building Democratic Armies in Africa, Asia, Europe, and the Americas* (Princeton and Oxford: Princeton University Press, 2012), p. 16.

20 Samuel Finer, *The Man on Horseback: The Role of the Military in Politics* (4th Printing) (New Brunswick and London: Transaction Publishers, 2006), p. 23.

21 Nordlinger, *Soldiers in Politics: Military Coups and Governments*, p. 2.

22 See Perlmutter, *The Military and Politics in Modern Times*.

23 Amos Perlmutter, "The Praetorian State and the Praetorian Army: Towards a Taxonomy of Civil-Military Relations in Developing Countries," *Comparative Politics* 1, 3 (1969): 382–404.
Moris Janowitz, *Military Institutions and Coercion in the Developing Nations* (Chicago and London: The University of Chicago Press, 1977), p. 91.
Renaud Egreteau and Larry Jagan, *Soldiers and Diplomacy in Burma: Understanding the Foreign Relations of the Burmese Praetorian State* (Singapore: NUS Press, 2013), p. 21.
24 Shah, *The Army and Democracy: Military Politics in Pakistan*, p. 2.
25 Samuel Huntington, *The Third Wave: Democratization in the Late Twentieth Century* (Norman: University of Oklahoma Press, 1991), p. 235.
26 See Alfred Stepan, *The Military in Politics: Changing Patterns in Brazil* (Princeton: Princeton University Press, 1971) and Alfred Stepan, "The New Professionalism of Internal Warfare and Military Role Expansion," in *Authoritarian Brazil: Origins, Policies, and Future*, ed. Alfred Stepan (London: Yale University Press, 1976).
27 Koonings and Kruijt, "Epilogue: Political Armies Between Continuity and Demise," p. 336.
28 Muthiah Alagappa, "Investigating and Explaining Change: An Analytical Framework," in *Coercion and Governance: The Declining Political Role of the Military in Asia*, ed. Muthiah Alagappa (Stanford: Stanford University Press, 2001), p. 52.
29 Barany, *The Soldier and the Changing State*, p. 3.

2 *Tentara rakyat* and *dwifungsi*

From Nasution to Suharto

*Muhamad Haripin, Adhi Priamarizki,
and Keoni Indrabayu Marzuki*

We mentioned in the previous chapter that Indonesian military formed an interventionist ideology to prevent outside parties meddling with the armed forces' internal affairs. Prior to Gatot's 'proxy war' and Ryamizard's *bela negara*, such thinking was primarily defensive in nature. This chapter aims to elaborate the utilisation of army thinking as a form of defence mechanism until the fall of the New Order regime.

As discussed previously, the Indonesian armed forces forged its tutelary belief as the country's 'guardian of the nation' by reflecting upon the protracted war of independence and revolutionary war (1945–1949), in which the military played a key role. Like other colonised countries in the world, Indonesia pretty much absorbed influences from its previous colonial powers, the Dutch and the Japanese. The impetus of the Indonesian military consisted of former Japanese trained officers, *laskar* (local militias), and a few former military officers from the Royal Netherlands East Indies Army (KNIL).[1] These three groups' different characteristics shaped the armed forces' core values, including how the military perceived its relationship with the civilians. KNIL was established in 1830 and primarily consisted of Dutch and Eurasian soldiers. But as with other colonial armies, KNIL also recruited a small number of indigenous Indonesian soldiers at first, particularly the predominantly Christian Ambonese.[2] The number of indigenous Indonesians soldiers swelled during World War II as an effort to resist the Japanese invasion to the East Indies. During the Japanese occupation in Indonesia, the Japanese formed the Defenders of the Homeland (Pembela Tanah Air: PETA) – a voluntary military unit formed to support Japanese imperial armed forces in opposing potential invasion from Allied Forces. The intensifying battles during the World War II forced the Japanese to organise local auxiliary security forces and paramilitary organisations, such as Heiho. According to President Sukarno, Japan wanted to cooperate with the native population in order to create friendlier inhabitants when the country fights its adversaries.[3]

The Japanese imperial army at that time trained PETA troops with an emphasis on *semangat* (spirit of combat) and guerrilla tactics rather than professionalism. PETA's basic military training focused largely to develop robust physical stamina, blind obedience to their colonial masters, as well as proficiencies of small arms and light weapons and a very limited knowledge on how to use heavy weapons or knowledge of military science.[4] In addition, the idea that victory was to be achieved not by cunning strategy but by the exercise of iron will and emphasise on the possession of a resilient mental attributes rather than formal military skills or material equipment became PETA's core belief.[5] The emphasis on mental indoctrination became a precursor for military disobedience towards the civilian authorities, given that fascist and anti-democratic values were an inherent part of the doctrine, which further leads to the reinforcement of the belief that the army is the "soul of the nation with superior position vis-a-vis the civilian."[6]

Besides the Japanese-organised PETA, there were also some local militias or *laskar* groups that became part of the fledgling Indonesian armed forces. *Laskar*, whose ranks and numbers proliferated after the war of the Indonesian national revolution, primarily consisted of local thugs and youths. Unlike PETA, these militias were driven by emotional, religious, and ethnic reasons, predominantly unorganised and partisan, which made them prone to politicisation.[7] The leadership of the country firstly formed the People's Security Body (Badan Keamanan Rakyat: BKR) following the declaration of independence with the focus to support the police in maintaining order. The BKR consisted of volunteers from former PETA members and other Japanese organisations as well as thousands of youths from the various *laskars*. The central government failed to establish a centralised command at the BKR as many of its members, particularly those affiliated with *laskars* and youths, involved in skirmishes with British and Japanese troops without direct orders.[8] On October 5, 1945, the poorly organised BKR was replaced by People's Security Army (Tentara Keamanan Rakyat: TKR), which was the embryo of Indonesia's national armed forces. Later, TKR became the Indonesian National Army (Tentara Nasional Indonesia: TNI) on June 3, 1947.

The army at that time also started to accept a small number of former Dutch-trained officers, and one of them was Oerip Soemohardjo, who later was installed as TKR Chief of Staff. Oerip and his colleague Didi Kartasasmita, also another former Dutch military officer, called other Indonesian military officers who were part of KNIL to join the TKR. Officers from the colonial army who eventually joined assumed top positions in the armed forces and the police. But the swelling number of former KNIL officers in the national armed forces fomented jealousy and disillusionment among former PETA officers and those *laskars*.[9] Unlike former PETA members and *laskars*, former KNIL members were taught to implement military professionalism (*beroeps militaire*) and to steer clear from politics. Following the disbandment of KNIL, about 26,000 out of 65,000 soldiers joined the ranks of the Indonesian armed forces, while the rest joined the Netherlands Royal Army or retired.[10]

The fledgling Indonesian army, having organised organically from different components of force, soon grew resentful towards the civilian government, which stemmed from two key events during the revolutionary period. The first was when Mohammad Hatta proposed the rationalisation of the Indonesian armed forces, which later triggered the so-called 1948 Madiun Affairs when he served as the prime minister. The rebellion was led by several military personnel with ties to the Indonesian Communist Party (Partai Komunis Indonesia: PKI) that felt disappointed towards the performance of Hatta's administration and disagreed with the rationalisation programme. This rationalisation effort to enforce civilian control towards the military ended disastrously and sparked a rebellion. The second event is the republican government's decision to surrender to the Dutch following its military offensive against the republic in 1948 – favouring diplomatic struggle instead of guerrilla resistance, as the armed forces preferred.[11] The republican government's action was perceived as a betrayal against the nation. In protest against the government, the armed forces – led by the charismatic General Sudirman – mounted guerrilla resistance, which subsequently demonstrated its independence from the civilian government. The detainment of leaders of the republic by the Dutch in December 1948 had further alienated the army from the central government. This contradicting approach between civilians and the military made the latter feel they have much to contribute to the nation than the others.

On March 1, 1949, the armed forces launched an offensive attack to Yogyakarta, which was claimed to be massively successful even though they only occupied the city for only a few hours. The army also apprehended the negotiations in 1949 with great suspicion and felt cheated by the terms of transfer of sovereignty in December 1949.[12] Although the military was willing to cooperate with the central government, many of its officers distrusted their civilian counterparts. Army General Sudirman became the symbol of the army's belief that it had higher noble status compared to the civilians, as Sudirman persistently refused to negotiate with the Dutch and follow negotiation settlement and opted to do guerrilla campaign.

Following the end of the revolutionary war, the 'military technocrats' camp took over the control of the Indonesian armed forces. They were very young when taking control of the TNI. Abdul Haris Nasution was in his thirties when he became army chief of staff in 1950, and Tahi Bonar Simatupang was also in his thirties at that time. The new generation of Indonesian military attempted to inoculate themselves from politics, but such an isolationist outlook did not last long as the 'complex circumstances contributing to the fluidity of the power structure' dragged the army back to politics. Turbulent national politics, particularly due to the instability in the national parliaments, and the army headquarters' struggle to handle rival factions in the different sub-regions of the archipelago had made factions within the military to ally with the civilian politicians to strengthen their positions.[13] One of the most glaring of this schism in the army was between the ex-PETA officers and the former KNIL officers in the early 1950s. General Nasution from the technocrat-professional faction of the army supported Hatta's armed forces rationalisation policy. As the army chief of staff, Nasution planned to reorganise and streamline the military, but his proposal apparently caused disgruntlement amongst former PETA members due to the concern that former PETA members would be side-lined in favour of officers with KNIL background given that PETA members were not as well versed in military affairs as their ex-KNIL colleagues. Compounding the schism further was the fact that the central command of the armed forces was dominated by former KNIL officers.[14] The schism culminated in October 1952, when parliament members had allied with ex-PETA officers demanding the removal of Nasution and his associates from the army leadership. In response, the military leadership perceived it as civilian intervention and reacted by organising a large civilian demonstration in front of the Presidential Palace, appealing the parliament to be dissolved, as well as pointing their ordnance towards the palace. President Sukarno did not budge and instead suspended Nasution, thereby defeating the armed forces' first open challenge to civilian authority.

In the early days of Indonesian military, the *laskar*, former Japanese trained officers, and former KNIL officers significantly influenced the Indonesian armed forces in many ways. The three groups' distinctive characteristics, values, and historical experiences are embedded into the ideology and organisational structure of the military. They definitely had suspicions towards each other, particularly towards the former KNIL officers, who were seen as colonial power collaborators. Despite their different backgrounds and thinking, those groups managed to melt into one entity – largely thanks to unifying figures and factors such as General Sudirman. The dissatisfaction towards the civilian and the military's tutelary belief became crucial factors that united those various groups within the armed forces. The military perceived itself as the guardian of the nation that has higher place than the civilian politician who opted to cooperate with colonial power rather than fight unwaveringly.

Nasution's *jalan tengah* and the army's *dwifungsi*

Experiencing first-hand how political instability during the liberal democracy era affected the army, Nasution was deeply concerned that the Indonesian military will evolve into civilian politicians' pawn or be used as leverage. Concurrently, however, he did not want his corps to take full control of politics like military regimes in some countries. Therefore, when he was redesignated as the army chief of staff for the second time, he proposed the *jalan tengah* ('middle way') concept while speaking at a graduation ceremony at the military academy in Magelang, Central Java, on November 1958, to avoid such a situation. In his speech, Nasution espoused his belief of what the TNI's role and position in Indonesian society should be: it should not be situated at the centre of power and monopolise the state, like some militaries in Latin America do, but on the other hand, the military should also be not the instrument of the government, like the militaries of Western countries. His proposition was that the Indonesian military should be a spectator in politics, but individual officers must be given a chance to participate in the government and to implement their non-military skills in developing the nation. According to Nasution's logic, this proposition requires placement of military officers in state institutions, including state-owned enterprises.[15] When Indonesia nationalised many of the Dutch business units in 1950s, Nasution installed numerous military officers as directors and/or chief executives of the companies in order to prevent PKI controlling the companies.[16] One notable example of military officers being installed in these nationalised Dutch corporation was Ibnu Sutowo, who later headed Pertamina (1968–1976), Indonesia's state-owned petroleum company.

The proclamation of the State of Emergency in April 1957 also contributed massively to the expansion of the role of the Indonesian military to civilian realms, particularly in the economy and politics. The expansion to civilian realms granted the army leadership with unprecedented access to vast sources of finance and patronage. In addition, the military galvanised its elite status within the society as civilian institutions suffered from efficiency issues and lack of political authority given the instability that engulfed the country during the Liberal Democracy period.[17] Realising that he needed to balance the growing influence of the military, President Sukarno forged a cordial relationship with PKI. Sukarno further developed the concept of 'Nasakom,' an acronym of *nasionalis, agama,* and *komunis* (nationalist, religious, and communist) in the hope to unite the dominant forces in Indonesian society and to create an equilibrium between the three factions. 'Nasakom,' in essence, was Sukarno's answer to the factionalism of parliamentary democracy and a necessity to bring stability during this turbulent period.[18]

Sukarno's flimsy triumvirate of Nasakom showed its cracks as the army and the PKI turning into the two most dominant political forces and started to clash with one another, while the religious group's influence waned. The final nail in the coffin for Nasakom came in 1965 with the allegedly attempted communist coup orchestrated by PKI. Following the event, the army, led by Suharto, took control of the situation and strengthened its political influence, as well as its prestige within the society by systematically purging the communist party followers and its sympathisers – which also includes a number of naval and air force officers who were allegedly communist sympathisers and officers deemed as Sukarno loyalist – with the collaboration of Muslim religious groups. Suharto's ascension meant that the army – the largest and the most politically influential of the three services – had the opportunity to devise the rules for others and determine the military structure on its whim.[19]

Ulf Sundhaussen noted various causes of the expansion of the Indonesian military to non-military fields. Commitment to economic modernisation and prevention of civilian infringement to its interests fuelled this expansion.[20] The army used its success in purging the communist to buttress the claim as the guardian of the nation. It also marked the rise of Suharto and his New Order regime. The combination of force, civilian fragmentation, economic decline, and manipulated public images of the new regime accelerated the entrenchment of New Order's rule.[21]

The armed forces and Suharto also started to consolidate its political power to strengthen their political position. The TNI put many of its officers to hold public offices at both central and local administrative levels. Systematic installation of military officers into state and civilian institutions, however, deviated from the middle-way doctrine introduced by Nasution, and this development spurred the realisation among the military leadership that they needed a doctrinal justification to keep the status quo. In a seminar in April 1966, the armed forces formulated a doctrine that paved the way for their involvement in political and economic development, their role as a guardian of the state ideology Pancasila, and their duty to uphold 1945 national constitution. They modified the middle-way doctrine and 'reinvented' it as *dwifungsi* (dual-functions) concept. The armed forces wanted a doctrine that can help usher in political and economic stability in the state, which was in turbulence following the 1965 chaotic period. The military thought that the people depended on the armed forces' capability to foster the development and bring prosperity for them. Therefore, it is TNI's duty to meet the people's need.[22]

The declaration of the new doctrine had given a strong justification for the military to be involved in day-to-day civilian duties, over and above its traditional function as a defence force. The military in the early 1970s dominated the political sector, the economy, defence, and other socio-cultural areas. These sectors are inextricably linked and contribute significantly to the armed forces' material power. The military's domination in politics, for example, opened new opportunities to access economic resources. Vice versa, control over the economy provided the military with patronage resources, which are useful to secure or promote their political interests. Effective control over these two sectors meant that the military had every measure necessary to protect its corporate interest, that is, to maintain its involvement in politics. The armed forces also became the backbone of Suharto's New Order regime, particularly in suppressing popular dissent, as well as the president's political opponents.

Dwifungsi under New Order

Even though the perpetrator and mastermind of the abortive communist coup of 1965 had never been conclusively determined, it was clear when the dust settled that Suharto benefited the most from the incident, having managed to skilfully exploit the chaos to his own advantage by taking over the country's leadership and establishing the New Order regime. While Sukarno employed populist mobilisation of political forces to consolidate national integration and pursue his adventurous domestic and international policies, Suharto opted to prioritise economic development and emphasised domestic stability. This gave an excellent justification for the military to strengthen its political control in the name of national stability, which was perceived to be an essential foundation for economic development and modernisation.[23] Moreover, the New Order regime constantly echoed the potential threat of communism and the mismanagement of the economy during the Sukarno years.[24] These narratives further legitimised the military's presence in politics and highlighted the importance of and necessity to implement dual-function.

Suharto cleverly orchestrated a political regime, with him as the apex of the pyramid and the principal patron for his clients. But Suharto, despite his military background, did not wish to rule as a direct military regime as he wanted to legitimise his rule, hence regular elections continued to exist in the otherwise authoritarian political system.[25] Golongan Karya (Golkar) – which consisted of three components namely the bureaucracy, military, and Suharto's crony – was his primary political vehicle to win elections and exercise hegemony for more than three decades. Apart from its sprawling 'party' structure and compelling civil servants to pledge loyalty to Golkar, Suharto also employed strong-arm measures such as using the military to intimidate and coerce political opponents in order to ensure the longevity of his hegemony. Suharto's former aide General Sumitro believed that the involvement of the military to help Golkar in winning elections was necessary.[26]

Under the auspices of dual-functions, Suharto put many retired and active military officers to various state-owned enterprises, bureaucracies, and other civilian institutions in order to solidify his personal patronage networks, as well as ensure the fidelity of these officers. General Nasution later criticised this as a deviation from the dual-functions concept itself.[27] Furthermore, Nasution perceived that the armed forces during New Order regime had been manipulated to benefit Suharto personally and sided with one particular group, which was Golkar, rather than standing above all groups. The army's sprawling territorial system also became a crucial tool of New Order regime to mobilise support for Golkar. Local commander often issued directives to local-level leaders, including mayors and regents, even though those local leaders were supposed to comply with the directives issued by provincial governor and Ministry of Home Affairs.[28] The late Lieutenant General (Marine) and former Jakarta Governor Ali Sadikin (1996–1977) disparaged and labelled the military as the Armed Forces of Golkar rather than the Armed Forces of the Republic of Indonesia due to this political mobilisation activity.[29]

The implementation of dual-functions not only weakened civilian supremacy and control vis-a-vis the military but also undermined its function as a defence force in different ways. First, the civilian became dependent on the existence of the armed forces to undertake basic functions of governance. The military, with its vast network and source, could easily take over duties within the purview of civilian institutions and appear as the dominant group, which robs the civilian institutions the opportunity to build organisational capacity. Second, the military strengthened its autonomy over civilian authorities as it had access to vast economic and financial resources outside the official budget allocation; thus the armed forces were less dependent on and less accountable to the government as they can have their own source of funding, thereby weakening the government control towards the military. Third, the military, preoccupied with non-defence affairs and day-to-day politics, neglected their primary duties as a defence force, as their secondary function took precedence over their defence function. Fourth, the armed forces became the authoritarian regime's tool, particularly to curtail political oppositions and suppress public unrest through violence or the threat of violence. Concurrently, Suharto's personalisation of the armed forces made it a subservient to the regime rather than the state's tool. Therefore, the military could conduct minor or gross violations with impunity as the regime allowed these transgressions as long as those things serve the regime's interests.

The fall of the Berlin Wall and the implosion of the Soviet Union, which brought an end to the Cold War, marked the decline of communism as an ideology across the globe. This constituted as a major problem for the military given that they had continuously used the narrative of the threat of communism as a part of their justification to enter civilian realms. But the armed forces were swift to adapt to the new geopolitical realities by coming up with the term 'New Style of Communism' (*Komunisme Gaya Baru*: KGB) to warn the country that the threat of communism was not entirely gone but rather transformed amorphously, thereby generating a new model of justification to keep its involvement in all aspects of life and, by extension, justifying the maintenance of dual-functions of the armed forces. This fear mongering manoeuvre was frequently recycled by the armed forces and the regime through propaganda such as the controversial *Pengkhianatan G30S/PKI* ('Treachery of the G30S/PKI') film and compulsory public airing of the film to remind the society about the communist threat and romanticise their contribution in the past in neutralising it.

It took more than half a decade later in 1998 for the dual-functions doctrine to be completely dismantled under military reform and the military's entrenchment from politics and different aspects of civilian life to be curbed. Indeed, in spite of the implementation of military reform measures under the *Paradigma Baru* ('New Paradigm') concept – such as the abolition of military faction in the parliament and the cessation of military personnel secondment to civilian institutions – there were some lingering issues regarding the army's territorial structure, military's business activities, impunity from law, secretive military justice system, and unclear definition of TNI's responsibilities.[30]

Nasution's idea of dual-functions, in what he conceptualised as *jalan tengah* ('middle way'), was to ensure that the military always had a role to play, or at least an opportunity to participate in statecraft and to have an influence in politics regardless of how Indonesian politics developed. Furthermore, Nasution's conception was underpinned by Sudirman's ideal that the military should transcend social and political groups and not take sides with any groups other than the military. The military as an institution must remain neutral, though its officers should participate actively in governing the country. What is known as *dwifungsi* under the Suharto regime, on the other hand, had corrupted Nasution's ideals by deliberately engineering the necessity for the military to support the ruling group regardless of the cost. The military, especially through its territorial command structure, became a tool of mobilisation to invigorate political support for Golkar and to occasionally silence any form of discontent and political opposition. Under New

Order, the military, as an institution, practically sided with the authoritarian regime.

Notes

1 Sukardi Rinakit, *The Indonesian Military After the New Order* (Denmark and Singapore: NIAS Press and ISEAS, 2005), p. 6.
2 Anthony Joes, *Resisting Rebellion: The History and Politics of Counterinsurgency* (Lexington: The University Press of Kentucky, 2004), pp. 129–30.
3 Cindy Adams, *Soekarno: An Autobiography, as Told to Cindy Adams* (Indianapolis, Kansas City, and New York: The Bobbs-Merrill Company Inc., 1965), p. 195.
4 Joseph H. Daves, *The Indonesian Army From Revolusi to Reformasi – Volume 1: The Struggle for Independence and the Sukarno Era* (CreateSpace Independent Publishing Platform, 2013), p 37.
5 Ruth T. McVey, "The Post Revolutionary Transformation of the Indonesia Army," *Indonesia* 11 (1971): pp. 131–176.
6 Daves, *The Indonesian Army From Revolusi to Reformasi*, p. 37.
7 Ibid., p. 44. Some *laskars*, such as Hizbullah, were formed on the basis of Islam as their ideology, whereas others, such as Barisan Banteng, is nationalist. There were also several leftist *laskars*, such as Laskar Rakjat and Laskar Merah, that were affiliated to Indonesian Communist Party (Partai Komunis Indonesia: PKI).
8 Ibid., p. 87.
9 Ibid., p. 89.
10 Jean Rocher and Iwan Santosa, *KNIL* (Jakarta: Kompas, 2016), p. 202.
11 Katharine McGregor, *History in Uniform: Military Ideology and the Construction of Indonesia's Past* (Singapore: National University of Singapore Press, 2007), p. 128; Salim Said, *Genesis of Power: General Sudirman and the Indonesia Military in Politics, 1945–49* (Singapore: ISEAS, 1992), p. 91.
12 Harold Crouch, *The Army and Politics in Indonesia* (Ithaca, NY: Cornell University Press, 1978), p. 27.
13 Ibid., p. 29.
14 David Bourchier, *Illiberal Democracy in Indonesia: The Ideology of the Family State* (New York: Routledge, 2015), p. 102.
15 David Jenkins, *Soeharto and His Generals: Indonesian Military Politics 1975–1983* (3rd Edition) (New York: Cornell University, 1997), p. 2.
16 Priyono B. Sumbogo, "Jalan Tengah dan Dwifungsi," *GATRA*, March 8, 1997.
17 Ruth T. McVey, "The Post-Revolutionary Transformation of the Indonesian Army Part II," *Indonesia* 13 (1972): pp. 147–181.
18 Robert Hefner, *Civil Islam: Muslims and Democratization in Indonesia* (Princeton: Princeton University Press, 2000), p. 44.
19 Evan A. Laksmana, "Rebalancing Indonesia's Naval Force: Trends, Nature and Drivers," in *Naval Modernisation in South-East Asia: Nature, Causes and Consequences*, eds. Geoffrey Till and Jane Chan (London: Routledge, 2014), p. 182.
20 Ulf Sundhaussen, *The Road to Power: Indonesian Military Politics, 1945–1967* (Kuala Lumpur: Oxford University Press, 1982).
21 Mietzner, *Military Politics, Islam, and the State in Indonesia*, p. 51.
22 Seskoad, *Doktrin Perdjuangan TNI-AD: Tri Ubaya Cakti* (Jakarta: Angkatan Darat, 1966), p. 10, quoted in ibid., p. 52.

23 Honna, *Military Politics and Democratization in Indonesia*, p. 9.
24 Ulf Sundhaussen and Barry R. Green, "Slow March Into an Uncertain Future," in *The Political Dilemmas of Military Regimes*, eds. Christopher Clapham and George Philip (Totowa: Barnes & Noble Book, 1985) quoted in I Gede Wajan Sardjana, *Civil–Military Relations: The Role of ABRI in Indonesian Socio-Political Life* (Master Thesis) (Monterey: Naval Post Graduate School, 1995), p. 31, http://calhoun.nps.edu/bitstream/handle/10945/31485/95Jun_Sardjana.pdf?sequence=1&isAllowed=y, accessed August 5, 2017.
25 Leo Suryadinata, "The Decline of the Hegemonic Party System in Indonesia: Golkar After the Fall of Soeharto," *Contemporary Southeast Asia* 29, 2 (2007): p. 34.
26 General Sumitro was one of Suharto's trusted aides during the early years of New Order regime. He was head of Kopkamtib (Operational Command for the Restoration of Security Order). Sumitro was kicked out from Soeharto's inner circle following the Malari incident in Jakarta (January 15, 1974, riot). Jenkins, *Soeharto and His Generals*, p. 37.
27 Stanley Adi Prasetyo and Toriq Hadad, *Jenderal Tanpa Pasukan, Politisi Tanpa Partai: Perjalanan Hidup A. H. Nasution* (Jakarta: Pusat Data dan Analisa Tempo dan Institut Studi Arus Informasi, 2007).
28 Ibid., p. 217.
29 Honna, *Military Politics and Democratization in Indonesia*, p. 29.
30 Crouch, *Political Reform in Indonesia After Soeharto*, pp. 153–174.

3 *NKRI harga mati, ketahanan nasional,* and MOOTW

Muhamad Haripin, Adhi Priamarizki,
and Keoni Indrabayu Marzuki

The previous chapter discussed the use of military ideology to defend the Indonesian military's internal affairs and prerogatives against external parties' intervention. While it focused on the era prior to the end of the New Order regime, in this chapter we examine the early reform period.

As briefly discussed in previous chapters, the political liberation movement initiated in 1998 has forcefully brought the military to adhere to democracy as the only game in town. This development, however, is by no means the end of military politics. Quite contrary, the army establishment, led by then TNI Commander General Wiranto, reiterated the old song of 'communist threat' to revert the political privileges the military once held during the authoritarian period. Over and above the supposed communist threat, there was also a proliferation of new agenda to 'defend the country from the threat of disintegration.' Following the collapse of New Order – marked by the resignation of President Suharto on May 21, 1998 – Indonesia also experienced a growing regional unrest against the central government. Voice of oppositions from troubled provinces, most notably Aceh, Irian Jaya (later renamed as Papua), and East Timor, emerged to demand independence. The threat of separation become more apparent when the referendum of East Timor in 1999 resulted in favour of pro-independence camp. Moreover, the crumbling centralistic Jakarta establishment had also witnessed the rise of ethnic conflict and interreligious violence in some regions, such as the violent clash between Dayaknese and Maduraese in Kalimantan, as well as conflict –between Muslims and Christians in Poso, Central Sulawesi, and Ambon, Moluccas – which left thousands dead, injured, and many more internally displaced. These series of unfortunate events have prompted the sceptics to lament that the archipelago was on the brink of disintegration. The term 'Balkanisation' – the fragmentation of the state of Indonesia to smaller independent states – was perceived by the elites as a real threat. It is now widely acknowledged, thanks to critical scholarship and media investigation, that the military as well as police have played no minor role in instigating such horrendous calami-ties.[1] Nevertheless, the dominant view during those years was apparently that the conflicts were believed to be socially driven and a manifestation of regional dissatisfaction with the central government, instead of a part of political subterfuge to undermine democracy and civilian leadership, emphasising deep-seated anxiety of the elites in Jakarta over 'democracy,' which was understood as a ruling by masses and, furthermore, undermined for its 'perceived' messy nature. In this context, it did not take long for the army establishment to reintroduce a political campaign and strategic thought highlighting the integration of state: the political imperative of maintaining territorial integrity.

What does the view tell us? How such a way of thinking was intro-duced? It is no secret that during early years of democratisation, or popu-larly known as *Reformasi*, the military was at least divided into two camps: those who were keen to initiate reform-oriented agenda – known from its key figures such as Susilo Bambang Yudhoyono, Agus Widjojo, and Agus Wirahadikusumah – and a group of top-level officers who attempted to inoculate the military from democratic pressure and external scrutiny. The key differences between these groups centred on substantial issues such as the military appointment in civilian executive position and parliament as well as the extent of army's role in domestic security. Nonetheless, when it comes to the threats of disintegration and how such dangers mani-fested through recurring social conflicts, the army establishment agreed to strengthen its presence and to reassert authority upon the belligerents. The deteriorating environment suggests that the police – now responsible for domestic security and the maintenance of public order – had been unable to de-escalate the conflict effectively; therefore, the military must reassert its role, leveraging on tactical experience and personnel capability, in handling social conflict on such grand scale. On another side, the civilian leadership of both President B. J. Habibie (1998–1998) and President Abdurrahman Wahid (1999–2001), when the violence occurred, had difficulties to impose meaningful political restriction upon the military in order to limit their manoeuvre. In this context, social conflict apparently has 'consolidated' the internal military, and in return, the military was also using the state of emer-gency as a powerful politico-strategic instrument for its own right. Under the catchy nationalist discourse of *NKRI harga mati* ('The Unitary State of Republic of Indonesia must be defended at all cost'), the military has put forth a daring and pretentious claim that their extended roles in political sphere could save the country from the danger of disintegration, but more tellingly, "by claiming its role of defending NKRI in the time of democracy, TNI believes that it can exercise a veto power in the relationship with the government and that it can retain a political say in rejecting pressures for reform."[2]

At its core, *NKRI harga mati* is a loaded concept and reflects the military's strategic concern on Indonesia's contemporary security landscape. The concept turned out to be an ideological vehicle for the military to meddle with the recently established norms of military professionalism in which TNI has only been assigned in 'defence' affairs (*pertahanan*), while the mandate to maintain order and security (*keamanan*) was handed over to the police. This division originated from the 1999 parliament decree to separate the police from military so that the former could autonomously manage its own posture, organisation, and force in accordance with the latest development of democratisation in the country. The National Police Force had been incorporated into the armed forces ever since the Sukarno period. Suharto administration then continued this practice, making the national police as sort of the fourth force along with army, navy (including marine corps), and air force. The police greatly welcomed the separation as they gained an immense institutional autonomy and policing authority.[3]

This development was, however, hardly appreciated by the military elites, particularly those who doubted the police's ability to conduct their new assignments properly; the police is considered as 'younger brother' that should be remained under the watch of 'big brother,' that is, the Indonesian army. Social conflicts in the early years of democratisation were then exploited to stir this sentiment. Police was considered to be too weak to handle the unrest across the archipelago. The security environment deteriorated, and therefore the military was supposedly to be deployed swiftly, especially after the suicide bombing in Bali on October 12, 2002, following which terrorism had begun to enter the official lexicon of national security discourse in Indonesia. In responding to this twin development of internal conflict and terrorism, the military argued that the exclusion of TNI from 'security' realm could no longer be maintained politically. The military's success to propagate this public campaign of an all-encompassing security outlook was reflected in the assertion of *operasi militer selain perang* (OMSP) or military operations other than war (MOOTW) in the Law on TNI.[4]

How does MOOTW relate with the advancement of the army ideology? The proliferation of MOOTW has allowed the military to blur the line between 'security' and 'defence' functions. Conceptually speaking, MOOTW is the application of military means for non-defence ends; meaning, the military could be deployed in a non-war yet life-threatening situation, notably civil war or social unrest, natural disaster or man-made disaster, and terrorist attack. Regional and international organisations, such as the Association of Southeast Asian Nations (ASEAN) and United Nations (UN), have provided a set of norms and code of conduct for the military to engage in such situations. However, despite its seemingly good Samaritan intention – which reflects a moral and liberal order – the translation and application of such novel doctrine in domestic setting apparently could produce a rather disparate outcome.

During the democratic consolidation era of President Susilo Bambang Yudhoyono (2004–2014), we have witnessed how MOOTW has been mobilised by TNI to justify the military's politico-institutional interests, notably the maintenance of territorial commands.[5] By using the Indonesian contingent participation in the UN peacekeeping, disaster relief operation abroad, and counter-terror mission, the military has fused 'military operations other than war' into its ideological arsenal to sustain the army presence as well as its indirect political influence. It has already become a new normal to justify the reawakening of military's 'social function' in the name of MOOTW; for example, we observed that *TNI Manunggal Masuk Desa* (TMMD) or 'TNI Works in the Village' programme – a legacy of New Order-era military programme which has been revived as a routine for personnel assigned in local command to participate in local initiative development, such as building roads, bridges, and irrigation – has also become an integral part of MOOTW. On a different occasion, the military establishment also introduced an interesting concept of 'environmental defence,' which will place military personnel at the forefront of conservation and climate change mitigation programme – even though we have yet to hear of any serious investigation over the allegation of military collusion in illegal logging business.[6] This new military role as the 'guardian of the environment' apparently has also exploited MOOTW as its political and strategic rationales: the logic is that TNI has a legal obligation to participate in any effort in tackling the damaging effect of environmental degradation that will endanger national economy as well as the public's general well-being.

Understanding how Indonesia perceive national security is also instructive, not only to contextualise *NKRI harga mati* and the military's MOOTW programmes but also to understand the underpinnings behind *bela negara* and 'proxy war,' how they emerge within the backdrop of democratisation, and why the military continues to subscribe to a distinctively insular outlook. To some extent, Indonesia's perception on national security is also essential to contextualise and further understand why the military continues to play a prominent role in non-defence affairs. To begin with, Indonesia subscribes to a holistic view of national security that is complex and multi-dimensional. Where the traditional concept of 'security' equated security with a nation's capability to defend its territory against external threats, Indonesia's views of security denotes and connotes all aspects of life, including ideological, political, economic, societal, and cultural security (officially abbreviated as *ipoleksosbudhankam*). In this context, national security also views that the preparedness to face other form of threats, such as political subversion and infiltration of values incompatible with the national ideology of Pancasila, is just as critical as external threats. While military might can counteract physical threats, developing *ketahanan nasional* (national resilience) is essential to mitigate the amorphous threats.

The legacy of a long struggle against colonialism, threats of societal fracture underpinned by Indonesia's ethnic and cultural diversity, socio-economic vulnerability, disadvantaged military power relative to its neighbours, the New Order regime's desire for stability, and the concern that domestic instability could result in external intervention influence its conception of the term. The Indonesian military leadership advanced the idea and it was officially introduced and endorsed as a national security doctrine in the late 1960s and early 1970s, respectively.[7]

Ketahanan nasional is officially referred to as the dynamic condition of a nation, integrally encompassing all aspects of national life. It highlights perseverance and tenacity, which enable the development of national strength to cope with all kinds of challenges, threats, obstacles, and disturbances originating from outside as well as from within the country, directly or indirectly endangering the national identity, integrity, survival of the state, and its national objective.[8] It is a concept that links together with developmentalism in nature, recognising the interdependent linkages between security, political stability, economic development, and social welfare and emphasising self-reliance through the means of maximising the use of indigenous resources.[9] National defence policies at least up until the end of the New Order era have been to strengthen all constituents of the nation and domestic political stability in order to obtain the capability to fend off threats, including free market capitalism and foreign ideologies, safeguard the whole way of life of the Indonesian nation, and sustain national economic development and regime survival in general.[10]

Ketahanan nasional primarily serves domestic purposes. State stability and internal security, within the parameters of Indonesia's notion of national security, are considered to be an integral part of the state defence itself and essential to maintain economic development.[11] But, on the other hand, *ketahanan nasional* has an external outlook, which links national resilience and the broader regional resilience. Indonesian strategic thinkers view that the domestic instability of each ASEAN member state would lead to broader instability in the region, which in turn would negatively affect Indonesia's own stability.[12] Operating under this logic, Indonesian leaders fervently promoted the necessity for each member state to bolster its own resilience so as to build a foundation for regional resilience – the sum of the national resilience of each ASEAN member state – which enables the member states to address common problems and maintain their wellbeing together by forming a chain against internal and external threats. In turn, regional resilience enhances not only national resilience but also the security of its member states.[13] Here we can see that 'national resilience' is actually an inherently insular outlook given its ultimate objective of maintaining national security, despite containing the deliberation of external strategic affairs.

As opposed to physical security threats that primarily revolve around military attack, *ketahanan nasional* is primarily composed of non-military aspects. Yet, the primary agent responsible to maintain national resiliency was none other than the Indonesian military, in collaboration with military-affiliated institutions such as National Resilience Institute (Lembaga Ketahanan Nasional: Lemhannas) as the military's think-tank and the intellectual developer of *ketahanan nasional* concept and strategies, as well as National Resilience Council (Dewan Ketahanan Nasional: Wantannas) as the president's assistant in implementing national resilience strategy. Just as *dwifungsi* provided a justification for the military to encroach on domestic politics, *ketahanan nasional* legitimised the Indonesian military intrusion in areas that are beyond the conventional defence affairs.[14] The difference, however, lies in *ketahanan nasional*'s comprehensive nature. If *dwifungsi* granted the military with doctrinal foundation and, thus, the legitimacy to participate in political processes, *ketahanan nasional* provided the military with the authority to play a role in determining the parameters of state ideology and the means to propagate it; to participate in economic development; and to play a role in domestic security, among a plethora of others.

The military's portion of *ketahanan nasional* is expressed through the Total People's Defence and Security System doctrine (*Sistem Pertahanan Keamanan Rakyat Semesta:* Sishankamrata), which aims to unite the broader Indonesian society with the military in waging territorial defence of *Nusantara* – the indivisible unity of the land and sea of the Indonesian archipelago, by employing various means of both conventional and non-conventional warfare.[15] Implicit to the doctrine is a defence-specific justification for the military's penetration in the society in order to mobilise economic, political, social, technological, and moral assets of the country, through the army's sprawling territorial structure, for the defence of the nation and to strengthen national resilience. In other words, *ketahanan nasional* – along with other ideological and historical elements that underpinned *dwifungsi*, such as the revolutionary war, the state ideology of Pancasila, *wawasan nusantara* (archipelagic outlook), and their subsequent interpretations/derivatives – not only serves as guidelines that shape Indonesia's strategic thinking but also gives the Indonesian military the opportunity to participate in the securitisation of *ipoleksosbudhankam* and therefore maintain their participation in areas not ordinarily considered relating to the military sphere.[16] Their continued involvement in these sectors is essential to maintain the nation's ability to weather various challenges to national security, both physical and non-physical as well as externally and internally.[17] Within the confines of *ketahanan nasional*'s logic, unabridged removal of the military from non-defence affairs, such as politics, ideology propagation and interpretation, and economic affairs, without an appropriate alternative substitute will seriously compromise *ketahanan nasional* and thus harm Indonesia's national security.

As with *dwifungsi*, *ketahanan nasional* is ultimately a product of Indonesia's New Order, and it had served as a basis for the military to justify its deep embeddedness within the Indonesian society and to legitimise the military's involvement in political, social, and economic affairs. Formally, *dwifungsi* is no more, as the military abolished the doctrine following the implosion of the New Order regime. But unlike *dwifungsi*, the notion of *ketahanan nasional* has never been completely revised or erased entirely from the defence and security lexicon of the Indonesian military and strategic thinking. Furthermore, much of the foundational idea of *ketahanan nasional* remains and continues to be propagated throughout the rank and files via the military's standard educational curriculum, as well as officer coursework that military officers undertook in Lemhanas before they could assume a position at the senior leadership level. Indeed, some aspects of *ketahanan nasional* have been re-contextualised to emphasise and reflect the TNI's withdrawal from politics and the non-participatory role of the TNI in day-to-day politics. Yet, the curriculum continues to include courses that are socio-political, rather than defence and security-oriented, in nature.[18] The relatively intact notion of *ketahanan nasional*, to a certain extent, continues to give the military the encouragement and justification to play a role in non-defence affairs – particularly those that relates to the maintenance of aspects pertaining to *ketahanan nasional*. Part of the reason why the TNI is knee-deep and highly committed to assist government programmes of food self-sufficiency (*ketahanan pangan*) recently is precisely because a self-sufficient Indonesia would be highly resilient against uncontrollable soaring food prices, which can lead to instability due to popular unrest.

With some respect, the TNI's continued involvement in different non-military aspects seems to suggest that there is some degree of ideological and strategic drivers that shape their behaviour in post-Suharto Indonesia. This includes forewarning the citizenry of an assortment of threats, including the threat of Balkanisation, neo-communism, religious radicalism, the excesses of liberalism, sexual promiscuity, unbridled capitalism, drug abuse, energy insecurity, and many others. This is because these challenges could erode Indonesia's resiliency by destabilising social harmony, economic sovereignty, and political stability and threatening the sanctity of Pancasila ideology – and thus, they constitute a threat, whether real or perceived, to the Indonesian nation. As the sentinel, it is therefore the TNI's moral obligation to dive into and maintain its engagement in non-defence affairs, regardless of whether or not such a course of action is deemed 'unprofessional' or perceived to be exhibiting an unhealthy civil-military relation.

While *ketahanan nasional* in of itself is ideological, it was heavily politicised to perpetuate the military's penetration in Indonesian society. During the New Order era, Lemhanas, the military's think-tank, was responsible in designing the National Vigilance Refresher Course (*Penataran Kewaspadaan Nasional* or Tarpadnas) initiative. The initiative was launched under the premise that Indonesia faced a constant threat of instability, an issue which only the military can remedy.[19] The ultimate objective of this initiative was to allow the military to project its involvement in politics and preserve its corporate interests in terms of its role as the guardian of the state. Indeed, today the TNI is no longer at the forefront of politics. Yet, *ketahanan nasional* continues to be the guiding principle in Indonesia's strategic thinking, thereby providing an avenue for the TNI to remain embedded in the Indonesian society even after their political function is formally abolished.

There are several notable examples of how *ketahanan nasional* helped the TNI to protect its corporate interests. Chief among them is the maintenance of the Indonesian army's manpower-intensive territorial command structure despite pressure and sound arguments to completely or partially abolish the structure.[20] The late Major General Agus Wirahadikusumah, who served as the assistant for General Planning to the Armed Forces Commander in 1999, threatened to fully dismantle the sprawling structure much to the irk of his fellow army officers.[21] In fact, the plan was so unpopular that it eventually led to the removal of Wirahadikusumah from his post due to overwhelming backlash from the army officer corps and political pressure towards the Abdurrahman Wahid administration (1999–2001).[22] There are several arguments that help explain why the discourse of reforming the army's territorial structure gathered so much controversy, ranging from internal factional rivalry within the army to the fact that the military's political influence is propped up by this particular command structure.[23] Part of the reason of why it is unpopular, however, is that the army's territorial command structure is an important mechanism using which internal security threats can be swiftly neutralised. Emasculating the structure, therefore, had a real potential of jeopardising the country's security and resiliency altogether – which ran counter to the foundational thinking of Indonesia's defence doctrine. The possibility of the breakup of the Indonesian state and the need to maintain order following the downfall of the New Order regime, compounded by stronger demands for political decentralisation and financial independence of the regions, help encourage this line of thinking.[24]

Apart from its strategic utility and providing a justification for the army to maintain such a high upkeep structure, the territorial command is also essential in enabling the military's extra-budgetary revenue generation in order to finance the gap between its operational needs and the defence budget. This includes benign activities, including renting out military vehicles, collecting fees for land use, and selling spare fuel and spare parts to borderline illegal and criminal activities, such as protection racket for businesses – both legal and illegal to levying unofficial taxes. At the local level, the army was engaged in a policy of 'communal provision' where local units raised revenue for welfare and operating costs for collective purposes. Inevitably, these practices left an enduring legacy of corruption that, despite the cessation of military's involvement in business practices, is difficult to eradicate.[25]

So far we have discussed the development of military politics during the democratic transition and consolidation era, and, more importantly, how ideology has played an important role in shaping the military attitude towards the new circumstance of open political system which allows free fight among civilian politicians but, on the other hand, expects the military should be out of such competition. The verdict has been clear, in which ideology remains a powerful political instrument of the military – the army, in particular – to protect and even advance its institutional interests, namely to resist any external reform pressure and simultaneously to expand the military's role in non-defence sector. Based on the discussion in this and the previous chapters, we can argue that the Indonesian military employed ideology as a defence mechanism against outside parties' attempts in meddling with the army's internal dynamics. In the following chapter, we will discuss the latest expression of army ideology in the democratic consolidation period: 'proxy war' and *bela negara*; unlike the ideology of the pre- and early reform period, these thinkings are aggressive in nature.

Notes

1 Indeed, the extent and nature of the military and police involvement are part of an on-going debate. Nonetheless, it is widely acknowledged that the dynamics of military politics during transition – i.e. the separation of military and police, and military withdrawal from formal politics – has affected the course, scope, and outcome of conflicts. On violence in post-Suharto's Indonesia and its debate, see John T. Sidel, *Riots, Pogroms, Jihad: Religious Violence in Indonesia* (Ithaca, NY, and London: Cornell University Press, 2006); Gerry van Klinken, *Communal Violence and Democratization in Indonesia: Small Town Wars* (London and New York: Routledge, 2007); Dave McRae, *A Few Poorly Organized Men: Interreligious Violence in Poso, Indonesia* (Leiden: Brill, 2013); Christopher R. Duncan, *Violence and Vengeance: Religious Conflict and Its Aftermath in Eastern Indonesia* (Ithaca, NY: Cornell University Press, 2013); and Yuhki Tajima,

The Institutional Origins of Communal Violence: Indonesia's Transition From Authoritarian Rule (New York: Cambridge University Press, 2014).

2 Jun Honna, "From Dwifungsi to NKRI. Regime Change and Political Activism of the Indonesian Military," in *Democratization in Post-Suharto Indonesia*, eds. Marco Bünte and Andreas Ufen (London and New York: Routledge, 2009), p. 242.

3 On the development of national police in early democratisation, see Muradi, *Politics and Governance in Indonesia: The Police in the Era of Reformasi* (New York: Routledge, 2014).

4 On the official definition and scope of OMSP or MOOTW, see Article 7 Paragraph 2 (b) of Law No. 34/2004 on Indonesian National Armed Forces (Undang-undang No. 34/2004 tentang Tentara Nasional Indonesia/TNI). See also Muhamad Haripin, *Civil–Military Relations in Indonesia: The Politics of Military Operations Other Than War* (London: Routledge, 2019).

5 On the TNI's military operations other than war during democratic consolidation period, see Haripin, *Civil–Military Relations in Indonesia*.

6 On environmental defence and its relation with the politics of MOOTW, see Chapter 4 of Ibid.

7 Muthiah Alagappa, "Comprehensive Security: Interpretations in ASEAN Countries," in *ASEAN Security Issues: Regional and Global*, eds. Robert Scalapino, et al. (Berkeley: University of California, Institute of East Asian Studies, 1982), p. 58.

8 Dewi Fortuna Anwar, "Indonesia: *Ketahanan Nasional, Wawasan Nusantara, Hankamrata*," in *Strategic Cultures in the Asia-Pacific Region*, eds. Ken Booth and Russell Trood (New York: St. Martin's Press, 1999), p. 213.

9 Donald Weatherbee, "Indonesia's Armed Forces: Rejuvenation and Regeneration," *Southeast Asian Affairs* (1982), p. 158.

10 For a concise discussion on *ketahanan nasional*, see Sebastian, *Realpolitik Ideology*, pp. 11–14; Desmond Ball, "Strategic Culture in the Asia-Pacific Region," *Security Studies* 3, 1 (1993): 61; Ralf Emmers, "Comprehensive Security and Resilience in Southeast Asia: ASEAN's Approach to Terrorism," *The Pacific Review* 22, 2 (2009): 161; Nicola Baker and Leonard C. Sebastian, "The Problem with Parachuting: Strategic Studies and Security in the Asia/Pacific Region," *The Journal of Strategic Studies* 18, 3 (1995): 21.

11 Damien Kingsbury, *Power Politics and the Indonesian Military* (New York: RoutledgeCurzon, 2003), p. 31.

12 Mochtar Kusumaatmadja, "Some Thoughts on ASEAN Security Co-operation: An Indonesian Perspective," *Contemporary Southeast Asia*, 12, 3 (1990): p. 163.

13 Nicholas Tarling, *Regionalism in Southeast Asia: To Foster the Political Will* (New York: Routledge, 2006), p. 138.

14 Kingsbury, *Power Politics and the Indonesian Military*, p. 31.

15 A. Hasnan Habib, "Technology for National Resilience: The Indonesian Perspective," in *New Technology: Implications for Regional and Australian Security*, eds. Desmond Ball and Helen Wilson (Canberra: Strategic and Defence Studies Centre, Australian National University, 1999), pp. 60–65.

16 Weatherbee, "Indonesia's Armed Forces: Rejuvenation and Regeneration," p. 150.

17 Honna, *Military Politics and Democratization in Indonesia*, p. 61.

18 John Bradford, "The Indonesian Military as a Professional Organization: Criteria and Ramifications for Reform," *RSIS Working Paper* No. 73 (2005): pp. 15–16.

19 Honna, "Military Ideology in Response to Democratic Pressure During the Late Suharto Era," p. 79.
20 See, Lex Rieffel and Jaleswari Pramodhawardani, *Out of Business and On Budget: The Challenge of Military Financing in Indonesia* (Washington, DC: The Brookings Institution, 2007), pp. 91–93.
21 See, *Indonesian Politics and Society: A Reader*, eds. David Bourchier and Vedi Hadiz (London: RoutledgeCurzon, 2003), pp. 306–308 for Major General Agus Wirahadikusumah's views on dual-function and the Indonesian army's territorial structure.
22 Marcus Mietzner, *The Politics of Military Reform in Post-Suharto Indonesia: Elite Conflict, Nationalism, and Institutional Resistance* (Washington, DC: East-West Center Washington, 2006), p. 27.
23 See, Rinakit, *The Indonesian Military After the New Order*, p. 35.
24 Evan A. Laksmana, "The Enduring Strategic Trinity: Explaining Indonesia's Geopolitical Architecture," *Journal of the Indian Ocean Region* 7, 1 (2011): p. 108.
25 Lesley McCulloch, "*Trifungsi:* The Role of the Indonesian Military in Business," in *The Military as an Economic Actor: Soldiers in Business*, eds. Jörn Brömmelhörster and Wolf-Christian Paes (New York: Palgrave Macmillan, 2003), pp. 94–124.

4 'Proxy war' and *bela negara*

The historical and political trajectory

Muhamad Haripin, Adhi Priamarizki, and Keoni Indrabayu Marzuki

Prior to discussing the concepts of 'proxy war' and *bela negara* in a more in-depth way, it is important to outline some important points and context regarding *bela negara* to provide a fuller understanding of the concept. *Bela negara* in the context of this book is the brainchild of General (Ret.) Ryamizard Ryacudu –the defence minister in President Joko Widodo's first term (2014–2019). Ryamizard is former army chief of staff (June 2002–February 2005) with notorious hard-line stance against separatist and rebellion groups in Aceh and Papua. He spent most of his military career on various major operational assignments, including East Timor. After retiring from military duty in 2005, Ryamizard reportedly continued to monitor developments in national politics. He maintains a close relationship with Indonesian Democratic Party of Struggle (Partai Demokrasi Indonesia Perjuangan: PDI-P) and its Chairperson Megawati Sukarnoputri. Ryamizard's father, the late Brigadier General Ryacudu – commander of the Tanjungpura Regional Military Command (Kodam XII) in West Kalimantan in the 1960s, was a staunch supporter of the Indonesian first president and Megawati's father, Sukarno.[1] In 2004, prior to be succeeded by Susilo Bambang Yudhoyono, President Megawati nominated Ryamizard to become TNI commander to the parliament.[2] However, Yudhoyono rescinded the nomination and nominated Air Chief Marshal Djoko Suyanto instead, making him the first ever air force officer to become the Indonesian military commander. Even though Ryamizard has retired from military duty, his opinions on national political development continue to reflect that of the army establishment of the post-New Order era. He remains a critical figure in national political scene and openly supports the maintenance of army's non-defence affairs.

The ascent of Ryamizard to a highly strategic position of defence minister invited strong criticism from major segments of civil society. President Widodo's decision was considered to be irresponsible given Ryamizard's unsettling views on human rights as well as his jingoistic stance against opposition groups. For instance, commenting on the killing of Theys Hiyo

Eluay, a leader of Papuan freedom movement, in 2001, Ryamizard said the perpetrator was a hero – instead of a murderer. Ryamizard was also infamous for his no-holds-barred approach against Free Aceh Movement (Gerakan Aceh Merdeka: GAM). He strongly disagreed with the effort taken by Megawati administration to pursue peaceful negotiation with the Acehnese rebel group. During his first days in office, Defence Minister Ryamizard Ryacudu has showed keen interests towards ideological development of Indonesian defence establishment. He took a drastic change to institutionalise *bela negara* within Defence Ministry and other agencies, as evident in the inclusion of a special chapter on *bela negara* in Indonesia's 2015 Defence White Paper.[3]

Bela negara, literally translated as 'defend the state,' is basically patriotism-boosting campaign.[4] Contrary to common perception, the concept of *bela negara* is neither founded nor initiated by Ryamizard. The ideas or agenda of it have been around since early 2000s. National constitution stipulates that Indonesian citizen has the obligation and the right to participate in defending the state. In line with the constitution, Law No. 03/2002 on National Defence (Undang-undang No. 03/2002 tentang Pertahanan Negara) further regulates the implementation of *bela negara* and puts it under the purview of national defence governance. Indonesian citizens could participate in *bela negara* through at least four main avenues: civic education, obligatory basic military training, voluntarily joining the armed forces, and other professional contribution.[5] The 2008 Defence White Paper provides extensive discussion on the historical background of *bela negara* and why it remains important to acknowledge such an important concept for defence system. To further institutionalise this patriotism-driven ideology, President Susilo Bambang Yudhoyono then issued a presidential decree to designate 19 December as '*Bela Negara* Day'. Every year, *bela negara* is celebrated with official ceremony and mass rally, followed by various public events involving various social organisations.

Under Ryamizard leadership, Defence Ministry becomes the leading agency in promoting *bela negara*; it provides the institutional basis and resources for reintroduction of national values. He underlined the importance of partnership among ministries and public as well as private organisations to reinforce basic values of Indonesian statehood into concrete action – so that every citizen from different sectors would have a 'proper understanding' of nationalism and patriotism. Ryamizard targeted to recruit a hundred million *bela negara* cadres from all over the archipelago and provided them with civic education materials as well as basic military training, such as marching.[6] Ryamizard's target is undeniably ambitious but not necessarily unattainable as the ministry encouraged all public institutions ranging from state universities to state-owned enterprises, as well as private organisations such as NGOs, at the national and local level, to register their members for training or actively participating in public seminar arranged by the ministry. This initiative has caused controversy and invited criticism. Opposing voices of *bela negara* argue that it has threatened the fabric of democracy upheld since the end of Suharto rule in May 1998. In socio-political front, one study argued that *bela negara* is "simply another way for the military to engage in national politics through the militarisation of the civilian population under the supposed rights and obligations when it comes to defending the nation."[7] Furthermore, it is quite predictable to see that along with unity and solidarity values conveyed in the name of *bela negara*, discrimination and hate messages – as well as violent threats – against minority groups, such as LGBT and Islamic Shiite, become part and parcel of the programme.[8] In January 2016, Ryamizard openly expressed his view that LGBT – with clear reference to its community or social aspirations – was a form of foreign countries' proxy war against Indonesia.[9] Adding to that criticism, this Ryamizard's 'mass-mobilising politics' would also be counterproductive for the country's national military modernisation plan – that is emphasising the procurement of selected cutting-edge defence hardware, rather than over-investment on personnel.[10]

There are valid and justifiable concerns about the militarisation of the *bela negara* ideology; a worrying trend of concerted effort on the side of government to outsource its coercive capability to civilian-vigilante groups is apparent. In early 2017, the Islamic Defender Front's social media account (Front Pembela Islam: FPI) posted pictures of their members who participated in military-style training of *bela negara* in Lebak, Banten province.[11] FPI has been infamously known as a religion-veiled vigilante group that frequently raids nightclubs, karaoke club, department store, and restaurants. The group often imposes their socio-religious aspirations through the use of violence and strong-arm tactics against ordinary citizen. After the publication of these photos, protests as well as criticisms against the Defence Ministry – for allowing the FPI members to participate in the session – were mounting in digital spaces as well as offline.[12] However, Lieutenant Colonel Eka Sundawan of Defence Ministry refuted the opposition, arguing that all social organisations in Indonesia have the rights to participation in the state-sponsored training, the FPI included.[13] Eka Sundawan then argued that the ministry has collaborated not only with FPI but with other civil society organisations as well, for instance the right-wing paramilitary organisations of Pemuda Pancasila and Laskar Merah Putih.[14] Defence Ministry's director of Bela Negara Directorate Rear Admiral M. Faisal stated that those who opposed the training involving FPI had misconstrued an important point that the state has the responsibility 'to develop the personal character' of individual FPI members, not the organisation as a whole.[15] M. Faisal asserted that they should be taught to appreciate and learn about the national ideology of Pancasila.[16]

Interestingly, there was a moment when the defence ministry and military headquarters seem to see the problem of FPI participation in *bela negara* training differently. Responding to this political brouhaha, the Indonesian military's spokesperson Major General Wuryanto eventually talked to media that the participation of FPI members in *bela negara* training is "not allowed."[17] He further extended that the ban applied as well in other regions and announced that all military command should restrain from providing such training to FPI. Nevertheless, it is reported that both Defence Minister Ryamizard Ryacudu and even TNI Commander General Gatot Nurmantyo apparently refuted the statement of Wuryanto, Gatot's own subordinates, simply by reaffirming the established 'inclusiveness' of *bela negara*. Ryamizard pointed out, "As long as we teach (the participants) good things, why not? Every citizen of the country must defend the state. And so must the FPI."[18] In line with the minister, General Gatot said, "All citizens have the right to defend the state," and FPI members are –indeed– not an exception.[19] It became clear that the statement of military spokesperson regarding the ban of FPI members was encouraged by early findings that the training in Lebak military command, where the photos posted in social media were taken, was conducted without prior notification to the higher command. If the training procedure was properly carried out, as exemplified by a similar training involving FPI members' in Madura (East Java) in 2014, Gatot believed that such unnecessary misunderstanding and confusion could have been avoided. In other words, the problem is essentially administrative in nature, not a political one.[20] This 'peaceful resolution' between Defence Ministry and the TNI seemed to magnify the anxiety of opposition camps facing the duumvirate Gatot Nurmantyo and Ryamizard Ryacudu.

From a comparative perspective, Ryamizard's initiative to intensively promote *bela negara* is unprecedented. Previous appointees during Yudhoyono presidency, Juwono Sudarsono (2004–2009) and Purnomo Yusgiantoro (2009–2014), are low-profile figures and they consciously restrained their ministerial policy based on a narrow understanding of defence, which covered only traditional aspects pertaining to defence affairs, such as military procurement and international cooperation. Both indeed had expressed, to some extent, alignment towards the military. Juwono, himself a prominent defence expert and a professor of international relations at the University of Indonesia, did not hesitate to be at the opposite side of his fellow civilian counterparts in civil society organisations regarding strategic matters related to the core interests of military.[21] Meanwhile, Yusgiantoro came from professional background and had served as minister of energy and mineral resources during Yudhoyono's first administration. He had won

Yudhoyono's trust to work together with TNI in accelerating military modernisation programme.[22] Juxtaposed with his predecessors, Ryamizard has demonstrated – or initiated – a different kind of leadership in the defence ministry. Therefore, it is probably sufficient to conclude that Ryamizard's military credentials and political proximity with Megawati, the leader of PDI-P, have sustained the proliferation of *bela negara* ideology without meaningful opposition within the government, let alone the parliament.

Next, we are going to discuss 'proxy war.' It is interesting to see an inter-generational collaboration on ideology between Ryamizard and Gatot. Ryamizard is a decade senior than Gatot, with eight years separating them when they both first started their military career. Despite their generational differences, they have a relatively similar background, having experienced similar rigorous and almost exclusively domestic military education, and both share similar outlook and line of thinking about threats to national security and the solutions to address them.

Gatot Nurmantyo's conception of 'proxy war,' though had gained more attention following his ascension into the highest military leadership, has yet to be formally ensconced as the army doctrine. No written, doctrinal document on 'proxy war' has been coming out from the army's doctrinal development body. So far, the ideology of 'proxy war' is mostly reflecting Gatot's individual assessment and aspiration on contemporary politics, on domestic, regional, and global levels, and how Indonesia fits in all of these spheres. Indeed, it is problematic and questionable to rigorously examine 'proxy war' as the army's principal guidelines or doctrines; nonetheless, through it we could see how one idea became popular while others evaporated. The ascendancy of General Gatot Nurmantyo from commander of Army Strategic Reserve Command (Komando Cadangan Strategis TNI Angkatan Darat: Kostrad) to army chief of staff (Kepala Staf TNI Angkatan Darat: KSAD) and at last the TNI commander has been an evidence that his personal quality and aspiration of 'proxy war' are apparently more than welcomed by both the political and military top-level elites. But, of course the important question is, as hinted in earlier section, why 'proxy war'? Why does the army leadership maintain the view that Indonesia is under attack of covert operation of foreign major powers? These questions will guide us through critical but – unfortunately – unexplored topic of post-Suharto's Indonesian military.

The first public mention of 'proxy war' could be traced back to March 2014.[23] Gatot, who served as the commander of Kostrad at the time, visited universities to give public lectures about the challenges of 'proxy war' in Indonesia and the role of students to prevent much calamitous effect of such an offensive. His understanding about 'proxy war' is akin to Cold War era proxy wars, which is defined as "an international conflict between two foreign powers, fought out on the soil of a third country; disguised as a conflict over an internal issue of that country; and using some of that country's manpower, resources and territory as a means for achieving preponderantly foreign goals and foreign strategies."[24] The foreign powers in question rarely fought head on with one another but rather use their allies to assault the enemy. The Korean War in the 1950s, the Vietnam War throughout the 1960s–1970s, as well as the Soviet-Afghan War from the late 1970s are some classic examples of how proxy wars between the United States and the Soviet Union unravel.

Reflecting upon some of the traumatic events and humiliation Indonesia had to endure in modern times, of which most strikingly was the independence of East Timor province in 1999 (later become Democratic Republic of Timor Leste), General Gatot Nurmantyo insisted that 'proxy war' is not a wordplay; it is happening before our own eyes. Furthermore, he argued that the international organisation and foreign governments finance non-governmental organisations to criticise and to advocate banning of national corporations for corruption or environmental damage allegations. Meanwhile, he opined that nothing was happening if such allegations were inflicted upon foreign companies. Gatot pointed his fingers several times at Australia as the main sponsor of Timor Leste's independence in order to gain access to Timorese natural resources. Taking all into accounts, Gatot argued that the government and Indonesian people should take an immediate action and reclaim the country back from foreign intruders. This set of discursive and rhetorical materials have become a standard proposition of the 'proxy war' ideology. Minor adjustments were usually added depending on the audience he spoke to; nevertheless, the basic idea still persisted. Next, we will discuss Gatot's 'proxy war,' underlining its main features and connecting it with the prevalent tradition of Indonesian army ideology.

To begin with, Gatot's 'proxy war' is deeply concerned with foreign influence and foreign intervention via a third party towards national affairs. It is argued that as history has shown, many foreign countries have always been interested with Indonesia's vast natural resources. Gatot mentioned the fact that many of national strategic assets, for instance crude oil exploration (onshore as well as offshore) and palm oil plantation, being dominated by multinational companies as a troubling situation that requires evaluation. This has created unequal relationship between the local people and business entities which have exploited Indonesia's resources for years. Aside from allegation of exploitation, the notion of 'proxy war' also frames the condition as tacit imperial rule of great powers against Indonesia. Gatot asserted that foreign countries compete each other to obtain access to Indonesia's natural resources through non-military means. Gatot also highlighted an important context of resource scarcity at the global level as the ultimate driver for foreign countries to take interest on Indonesia and, by extension, to gain unrestricted access to her natural resources.

Foreign domination, xenophobia, and foreign infiltration are salient features of Gatot's 'proxy war' theory and are hardly novel in Indonesian political discourse. The sentiment of 'Indonesia is in danger' shares the core belief held by early Indonesian leaders who view the country as a 'pretty maiden' that is being courted upon by multiple suitors.[25] Indonesia is a 'great country' because of its natural resources, cultural richness, and so on; therefore, it is no wonder why Western countries colonised the archipelago since the 17th until the 20th centuries and looked for a way to do the same in modern times. Subsequently this idea influenced how the army establishment perceived the outside world as well.

Along with the Dutch and Japanese colonial power, the army also found its enemy in Marxism. The ideology is considered to be of non-Indonesian origins; therefore, the people should exercise caution not to be influenced by this imported idea. It is argued that the country had already suffered because of the communist-instigated rebellions in the early 20th century (1926 during Dutch colonial rule), 1948 rebellion in Madiun, East Java – three years after the proclamation of independence – and 1965's abortive communist coup.[26] Aside from concrete political challenges the Indonesian Communist Party exerted against the army, the antagonism against communist ideology was partly coming from deeply ingrained xenophobia sentiment and inferior mentality. Communist party succeeded to recruit members and sympathisers from all walks of life, although the majority of them came from peasants and industrial workers background; not to mention they also enjoyed cordial relationship with President Sukarno. However, the army was eventually able to end the communist ascendancy. The kidnapping and murder of army generals on September 30–October 1, 1965, turned the balance of power in favour of the military against the communists.[27] The latter, for the most part, was accused to have instigated such atrocities: that the communist made an attempt to stage a coup d'état against Sukarno.[28] General Suharto, then commander of Kostrad, was leading the concerted effort to undermine communist influence not only within the executive as well as legislative branches of government but also on its grassroots base. As soon as the army leadership under Suharto completed its political and organisational consolidation, the communist power in Indonesia collapsed, both politically and socially, particularly since the massive purge of its sympathisers in post-September 1965. It is widely reported that thousands (even millions) of communist party members and sympathisers, notably in Java and Bali, were detained without due process, tortured, and murdered.[29] Oddly enough, it seemed that New Order was frequently reviving the 'spectre of communism' to legitimise their politico-security rule in the society; they had exploited 'communism' as a powerful political discourse, and therefore the Marxist legacy could never be entirely wiped off from the archipelago.[30] Here, in this context, we will explore the re-awakening of old threats, including communism, and civil-military relations in contemporary Joko Widodo presidency that help us to explain further proliferation of General Gatot's 'proxy war.'

Looking at the current regional security predicament, notably the rising escalation of territorial dispute in South China Sea as well as potential major terrorist attacks in the region, it is difficult to deny that a highly vigilant outlook such as the Gatot's 'proxy war' could have currency among the political elites and public in general. The idea itself has fitly translated the social anxieties upon regional uncertainty and the possible major outbreak in the region, and, not to mention, its effect towards not only the conflicting parties, notably China, Vietnam, and the Philippines, but also the non-belligerent ones, such as Indonesia. Through simplification of 'proxy war' and its contextualisation upon historical national contexts, the army has weaponised the Indonesian polity with powerful counter-discourse against any potential as well as imminent threats, both domestic in origin and from abroad. In order to understand why an all-encompassing defence concept such as 'proxy war' could gain prominence and be promoted by high-ranking army general, we should be contrasting these security concerns with the actual national capability to address all those problems, which is – quite expectedly – insufficient.

As admitted by Ryamizard himself, the Indonesia's defence equipment, ammunitions, and logistics would not even last a week in a major conflict against other countries.[31] In this regard, lack of energy security (e.g. oil supply) is argued to be a major problem. The national military budget also remains below regional standard; this situation, in return, has made Indonesian military modernisation programme lag behind compared to other countries in the immediate Southeast Asian region, as well as the greater Asia Pacific. In this context, the country is experiencing something that could be called 'identity clash' or capability disparity. On one side, particularly throughout Susilo Bambang Yudhoyono administration, the public often heard international praises about Indonesian achievement in political and economic sector. The country is called as 'emerging democratic power' and a resurgent 'Asian giant';[32] Indonesia is also frequently attributed as the natural leader of the ASEAN and the largest Muslim country with democratic system. But on the other hand, as discussed earlier, Indonesia has suffered from serious lack of military capability and political leadership to drive away the region from potential warfare. In addition to that, domestically speaking, this gap has also deeper and frightening consequences. It has helped the birth of 'new nationalism' that its main features include inward-looking outlook and suspicions towards anything that is foreign in origin.[33] This wide gulf between the reality, the challenges the country encountered, and the public image being established lately is one important factor that increases the popularity and public reception of Gatot's 'proxy war.'

How is proxy war and its devastating impacts to the public manifested in everyday lives? Or to be precise, how the army establishment and General Gatot Nurmantyo explained a complicated concept of 'proxy war' to general population? Ironically, despite meaningful efforts to depict 'foreign infiltration' as a serious threat, Gatot himself had to borrow an English-based concept, 'proxy war,' to introduce the potentially devastating nature of the threat itself.[34] One might expect that Gatot would provide a down-to-earth proposition of a national threat he called 'proxy war,' but no such effort was ever made. On the contrary, he was looking no further to already known and widely reported cases as references, instead of discussing the concept in a rigorous way. In this regard, 'proxy war' was explained via its 'symptoms' or direct predicament. This method had been employed to popularise the term and make it closer to the public – at least that's how the attempts were meant for. Table 4.1 provides a list of the symptom of 'proxy war' in Indonesia, as stated by General Gatot Nurmantyo from various sources.

This list of symptoms is by no means exhaustive in nature, yet it displays the wide-ranging army's conception of domestic security challenges. We can easily see how, according to Gatot, 'proxy war' relentlessly assaults the archipelago in different forms: from direct intervention as exemplified by the case of East Timor disintegration to spreading distribution of pornographic materials among youths and promoting sexual promiscuity as a normalised custom. In this light, the table shows that Gatot's span of attention upon the danger of 'proxy war' was apparently not limited to three traditional sectors of secessionist movement, inter-group conflict, and manipulated or Western-funded mass demonstration, as reported previously.[35] He also greatly paid attention to diverse social phenomenon and contextualised it in accordance with 'proxy war' framework. It seems that no existing social and economic problems could escape from this ostensibly useful and all-encompassing ideological compass.

For some, the diagnosis looks convincing and sufficient to build containment agenda to isolate further damages to Indonesia's national security. Many notable civilian figures subscribe to this argument, whether partially or in its entirety, and launch their analysis of political situation precisely from this all-encompassing concept of threats. A respected and notable Islamic scholar from the Syarif Hidayatullah State Islamic University, Jakarta, Professor Azyumardi Azra, for instance, dedicates two long articles

Table 4.1 Symptom of 'proxy war' in democratising Indonesia

No.	Symptom of 'proxy war'	Argument/allegation of the military
1.	The referendum of East Timor in 1999 – later become independent country of the Democratic Republic of Timor Leste	Australian government was behind Timorese secessionist movement given its strategic interests to acquire access towards natural resources, especially hydrocarbon in Timor Gap.
2.	Control over national media by Western power	General Gatot Nurmantyo complaint about the absence of official media that could bridge the government and public. The existing media have been, he argued, infiltrated by Western interests to spread fake news and misinformation.
3.	The growing role of non-governmental organisations (NGOs)	These organisations receive funding and assistance from the United States and European countries. Therefore, according to Gatot, it is logical to suspect that their advocacy serves the purposes and interests of the Western power.
4.	Intensifying protests and demonstrations against national-owned palm oil plantations	Gatot wondered why many national companies were rejected by social activists in the region, while only few foreign companies received similar treatment. He suspected that these activists were hired and planted by foreign corporations and/or governments, thus creating this 'double standard'.
5.	Energy competition among nation-states	Gatot was frequently mentioning about the possibility of 'resources war' among sovereign states. The decline of global oil reserves fuels the desire to explore and gain access to new reserves, particularly those located in Indonesia.
6.	Terrorism	Gatot refuted the general understanding that the root of terrorism is injustice. He argued that terrorism was a direct result of energy competition. This logic, according to Gatot, explained the rise of Daesh (Islamic State of Iraq and Syria/ISIS or Islamic State/IS) in the Middle East.
7.	Past conflicts in West Kalimantan and Moluccas	The violence was argued to be a manifestation of 'proxy wars' in early Indonesian democratic transition period.
8.	Provocative news coverage	Provocative and tendentious news will harm social cohesion. The public is suggested to be careful and critical towards the media.
9.	Street fighting/gang fighting	It promotes disintegration and disunity that will benefit foreign power in dominating the archipelago – akin to the *divide et impera* tactic that colonial powers in the 17th century used to control Indonesia.

(Continued)

Table 4.1 (Continued)

No.	Symptom of 'proxy war'	Argument/allegation of the military
10.	Youth and student brawls	It deteriorates the Indonesian young generation; they will be segregated based on meaningless classification, particularly school origins. In one or the other way, great powers will tremendously exploit this unfortunate situation for their own interests.
11.	Drug abuse among youths and students	In line with the government's major anti-drugs campaign, the army takes stern view against the distribution and abuse of narcotics. In one occasion, Gatot even felt a need to mention about the devastating impact of drugs, 'Opium War' in mid-19th century, towards the Chinese people.
12.	Low enthusiasm of reading/low illiteracy	General Gatot Nurmantyo argued that the domination of media by few people has resulted in low enthusiasm of reading among Indonesian young generation. It is indeed quite problematic to trace relations between illiteracy issues with 'proxy war,' however he made comment about it.
13.	Distribution of pornography contents and free sex among youths	Pornography and sexual promiscuity are considered as major problems by the army establishments as these practices represent moral decadence of young generation, not to mention that it will cost the future of the country.

Source: Compiled by the authors from various public documents

on 'proxy war' and its impacts. His concern is particularly related with the influx of radical teachings of Islam that could derail the social cohesion of Indonesian society.[36] He asserted the need of political and social integration against the growing threats of 'proxy war.'[37] Along with prominent scholars, some renowned members of parliament also expressed their agreement with Gatot's 'proxy war.' They shared similar resentments against foreign infiltration and agreed that comprehensive approach should be deployed, not to mention military involvement, in such crisis. Tantowi Yahya, deputy head of Commission I – responsible for defence, foreign affairs, intelligence, and communication matters of 2009–2014 National Parliament (Dewan Perwakilan Rakyat: DPR) – argued that the Indonesian military should prepare for a new form of warfare in the 21st century, notably the threat of 'proxy war.'[38] His line of argument is similar with General Gatot's view on the subject discussed. Finally, Mahfudz Siddiq, head of commission I DPR – an experienced politician from Prosperity and Justice Party (Partai Keadilan Sejahtera: PKS), an Islamic-based political party – reiterated the importance of national vigilance in confronting new global challenges. Siddiq argued that Indonesia has been greatly threatened by unfavourable security circumstances – such as, the escalating tension of border dispute in South China Sea and its potentially devastating impacts that could spill over into Indonesian territory; non-traditional threats, such as terrorism, cybercrime, as well as separatism; economic warfare against foreign countries; and environmental degradation.[39] Quite expectedly, the concept of 'proxy war' was underscored to frame all these four pressing problems.

The prevalence of 'proxy war' narrative among the military does not wane following the end of Gatot Nurmantyo's tenure as TNI commander and his service as a military officer. His successor, Air Chief Marshal Hadi Tjahjanto (TNI commander, 2017–present), despite his air force background, seems to concur with Gatot with regard to the threats of 'proxy war.' In his confirmation hearing, Hadi outlined that the threats facing Indonesia in the immediate future are asymmetrical, hybrid – both military and non-military threats, and delivered via proxy. To be fair, 'proxy war' is but one of many aspects that Hadi highlighted at his confirmation hearing. The former Air Force chief of staff also described different forms of threats to Indonesia, such as cyber warfare, the evolving threat of terrorism, illegal fishing, and China's growing assertiveness in the South China Sea.[40] While the new TNI commander frequently mentioned about 'proxy war' in many of his speeches, Hadi Tjahjanto rarely dealt on the subject and placed greater focus on asymmetric warfare – a type of warfare where the actors might be of non-state origin. Unlike his predecessor, Hadi offers a relatively more concrete agenda for the TNI, such as enhancement of network-centric warfare capabilities, development of an integrated defence force, and development of an adaptive defence force, for the military in addressing the myriad of threats that Indonesia encounters.[41] But nevertheless – and despite the departure of Gatot from the military, large-scale rotation in the army leadership following Gatot's retirement and the ascension of Hadi – the military continues to advocate the threat of 'proxy war' to the Indonesian public. Furthermore, and as evident during Gatot's leadership of the military, all three services of the military have been focusing on the threats of 'proxy war.'

***

Ideology comes to serve certain political missions. 'Proxy war' and *bela negara* are not exceptions. Nonetheless, compared to the previous period of governance, as discussed earlier, the proliferation of recent 'proxy war' has demonstrated a rather interesting picture of the inner thinking within the army branch of TNI. In order to examine this important topic, we would like to present the following two follow-up questions to guide our discussion. Why does the army advance this inward-looking ideology amidst relative stable national political situation and economic development?

President Susilo Bambang Yudhoyono left his presidency with modest political and economic achievements. His two-period in office has indeed generated mixed reviews, but taking all into account, Yudhoyono was considered to have passed on a relatively good foundation for his successor, Joko Widodo.[42] Furthermore, why does *bela negara* and 'proxy war' discourses emerge when civilian control seems to be consolidated? A consolidated democracy will demonstrate a degree of reservation of the military's intervention in non-defence sector due to not only political constraint but also strategic necessity; meanwhile, a politicised army would harm the core organisational capability, which is to combat in warfare.

At this point, it is important to expand the discussion beyond personal politics. Even though the duumvirate of General Gatot Nurmantyo and Ryamizard Ryacudu is the main promoters of 'proxy war' and *bela negara*, their actions should be understood along with the military politico-structural context. Their behaviours both influence and, in retrospect, were influenced by the dynamics within the Indonesian polity. It is argued that the nationwide promotion of 'proxy war' has been highly influenced by the internal army interests to expand its domestic security roles.[43] The military's attempt to warn the public about 'proxy war' is part of a greater purpose to have a more meaningful role, as well as well-regarded domestic functions, including law enforcement in the case of counter-terrorism. At the politico-strategic level, the increasing status and position of military could be well leveraged into concrete political influences and economic advantages. The military has lost most of its domestic grip ever since the Indonesian National Police (Kepolisian Negara Republik Indonesia: Polri) was assigned in public security and law enforcement tasks – as regulated in Law No. 02/2002 on Indonesian National Police.[44] Meanwhile, the military has primary obligations to protect the country from external threats, or 'external defence' function. This legal and conceptual distinction has caused a great loss for not only the military's socio-political prestige but also most of its off-budget revenues from either legal, semi-legal, or illegal economic activities. It is indeed logical to conclude that the contextualisation and application of 'proxy war' into Indonesian political grammar supports the military case against the delineation of 'defence' and 'security' sector.

Socio-political factor, more precisely the society's viewpoint towards the military, also plays a role to explain as to why *bela negara* and 'proxy war' not only emerge but also flourish in the democratic consolidation era. In recent years, the public's trust towards the military has considerably improved. As reflected in some polls, the public highly regarded the TNI as one of the most trusted state institutions in the country – far beyond the police and the national parliament. As reflected in a survey released by Saiful Mujani Research and Consulting in May 2017, the TNI has topped the chart when it comes to public trust for over more than a decade – or more precisely since it underwent a large-scale reform. Other polls similarly indicate the high level of public trust towards the military.[45] The circumstances cannot be any more different than at the onset of *Reformasi*, when the public trust towards the TNI was at its nadir. In fact, one of the reasons why the TNI underwent reform was because the TNI leadership, under the command of General Wiranto, was highly sensitive to poor level of public trust towards the military, which was propped up by the revelation of TNI's complicity in human rights violations in Aceh and East Timor, as well as its role as the New Order regime's favourite tool of repression.[46] High level of public support towards the TNI means that the public would be easier to accept and less likely to resist ideas from the military, including 'proxy war' and *bela negara*.

Furthermore, 'proxy war' has also been examined as a response to President Joko Widodo's 'global maritime fulcrum' concept.[47] Jokowi promotes a new approach to reorient Indonesia's general outlook from a land-based internally focused outlook to a maritime-focused outlook (see Figure 4.1).[48] Both domestic and international audiences welcomed this development as it provides a better narrative that suited Indonesia's geostrategic character as a maritime nation and provides directions for economic development, as well as new opportunities for security partnership. But other countries in the region expressed some concerns regarding this outlook shift as well. The Indonesian government had begun to take a sterner approach against illegal fishing vessels that operated within Indonesia's maritime territory. Vessels of Vietnamese, Thai, Malaysian, and Papua New Guinean origins were confiscated and scuttled after they have been found guilty for illegal fishing activities.[49] In defence sector, the 'global maritime fulcrum' naturally favours the Indonesian navy or TNI Angkatan Laut, with possible shift in Indonesia's procurement focus and additional budgetary allocation.[50] This policy reorientation has stirred controversy within the TNI as the shift potentially alters the balance within the military to favour the navy and to some extent the air force, most likely at the expense of the army. Against this backdrop, 'proxy war' must be propagated intensively to maintain the army primacy over other branches in TNI.

These assessments have provided a detailed analysis on the rationales behind 'proxy war'. Nonetheless, they have yet to inform us regarding the relations of the ideology with current civil-military relations. Framing the 'proxy war' as an instrument to reassert the army rule is useful and informative; however, it tends to downplay the power projection of such politically offensive ideology. In the previous section, we have discussed how *dwifungsi* ('dual-function') emerged and is being institutionalised as the military's most salient socio-political features in the authoritarian New

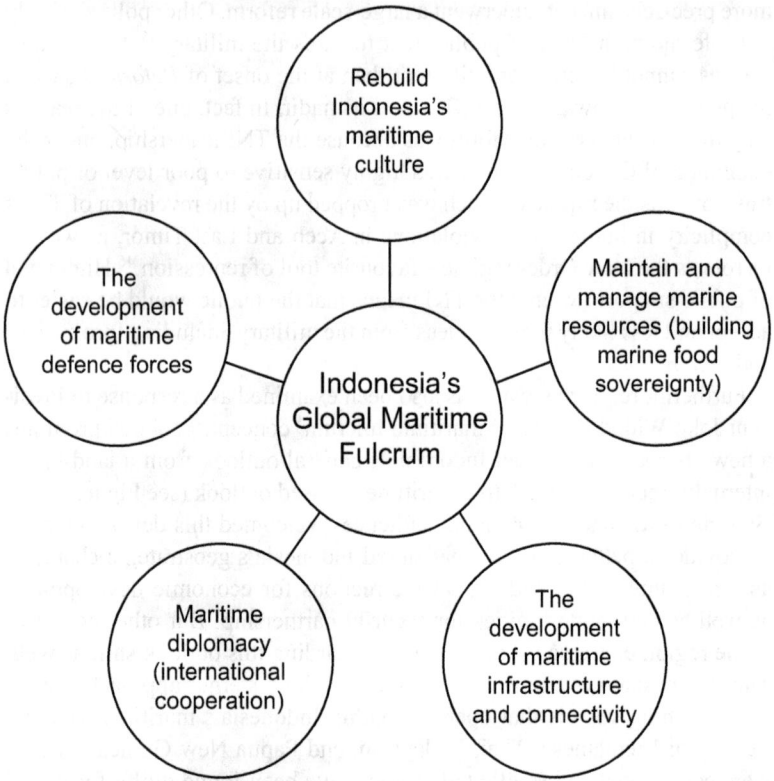

Figure 4.1 Indonesia's 'global maritime fulcrum'
Source: The authors

Order period. The army was operating as the 'agent of development' that directly participated in day-to-day political as well as economic endeavours; the officers and military retirees were installed as governors, mayors, or regents and directors of state-owned corporations. Furthermore, during the initial years of democratisation, *NKRI harga mati* had been introduced as a response to undermine a worrying trend of disintegration, as exemplified by the referendum of East Timor in 1999. Unlike previous doctrine and narratives that emerged following a crisis and instability, 'proxy war' and *bela negara* occurred in an era of democratic consolidation.

How does this happen? The current governor of National Resilience Institute (Lembaga Ketahanan Nasional: Lemhanas), Lieutenant General (Ret.) Agus Widjojo (2016–present), offers an interesting perspective. *Bela negara* and 'proxy war' are indeed a symptom, but not in a sense that is understood by General Gatot Nurmantyo; it is a symptom of the reawakening of the politicisation of military. He reasserted, "The military should not be expected to conduct reform voluntarily."[51] According to him, the root cause lies within the military establishment itself: the half-hearted internal reform effort the military had undertaken during the onset of *Reformasi* left chances for the momentum to reverse the achievement previously gained in early democratisation. Widjojo also partially blamed civilian authorities due to its indecisiveness and over-reliance towards the uniformed officers for not only support and legitimacy in political power game but also for policy implementation and programmes. Indeed, civilian leaders, such as ministers, governors, and mayors among others, frequently partnered with the military to help address some stumbling blocks that plagued policy implementation. In recent years, the Ministry of Agriculture has sought the aid of the TNI to assist them with food self-sufficiency programme, whose tasks range from distribution of seeds and farming equipment to monitoring harvest results, among others. Thanks to the military's sprawling territorial network, the ministry can execute the programme in a more comprehensive manner and more effectively – while subsequently gaining quick wins in order to boost their standings.[52]

Agus Widjojo's insight is instructive; however, it has yet touched the structural problem. Many have come to agreement that civil society and the political elites' support for further military reform is stagnating. But how does this problem manifest in Joko 'Jokowi' Widodo's first term of presidency? How does it affect the relation between president and military?

President Widodo seems to be fully aware of his limitation in upholding civilian supremacy. In his early days in office, he was immediately caught up in the elites' tug of war for cabinet and other strategic positions. His decision to abort the nomination of Police Commissioner General Budi Gunawan – a close ally of Megawati Sukarnoputri, the matriarch of PDI-P, which is also the political party that the president is a member of – as the head of Indonesian National Police (Kepala Polri: Kapolri) has put a test on the president authority. In the following passages, we will discuss how Jokowi and PDI-P temporary political standoff has affected the political configuration of the president and the military, which in effect encouraged the proliferation of 'proxy war' and *bela negara* ideologies accordingly.

First of all, we need to note that President Widodo has somewhat complicated relationship with his own supporting party. Rather than positioning himself as 'loyal cadre' who would follow party directives, including on the assignment of ministerial posts, he apparently took the matters into his own hands. The legal structure is enabling such a degree of autonomy since Indonesia implements direct presidential election system since 2004, in which the candidates are competing for the votes of population, leaving the party as the gatekeepers to nominate candidates and campaigning machine. Nonetheless, politically speaking, as obviously seen in other democracies, the role of parties in presidential election is by no means diminishing; they have an organisational structure and financial power to support the candidates, either in national or local level. On the other side, Jokowi's popularity has increased significantly and became the main appeal for voters to choose PDI-P – rather than otherwise (we know this phenomenon in election and political party studies as 'coattail effect'). Against this background, Widodo's move to distance himself from PDI-P generated some anxieties and uneasiness among high-ranking figures in PDI-P. The relation between the two got worsen when the president eventually backpedalled on his nomination of Budi Gunawan. This decision was believed to be provoked by the report of non-governmental organisations and media outlets of Gunawan's financial irregularities where his personal wealth has been exceptionally higher above his peers in national police. The president was politically attacked for this cancellation, and it subsequently negatively affected the institutional cohesion of national police as well.

Against this backdrop, Jokowi then began to demonstrate alignment with the military establishment. He was searching for support and loyalty of the institution during political crisis. One military officer explained, "Jokowi is clean and humble but he's weak and he doesn't have backup from elsewhere in the system – that's why he turns to the army. We've never had a president who visited military units six times in his first year."[53] This suggests that it was Joko Widodo, a civilian president, who has invited the military to reassert its influence over the civilian polity. And, it also shows the extent of the army's political resilience against civilian democratic consolidation.

Second, President Widodo is known – and considered himself as well – as an 'outsider' of national politics. He comes from a humble background, graduating from a respectable public university and working as self-employed businessman for years. It was only after he decided to run for mayor of Surakarta, a small but vibrant city in Central Java, that he began to gain national-level renown. His popularity skyrocketed when he eventually won the 2012 gubernatorial election in Jakarta. Despite his meteoric rise, Jokowi remains a new player within the established Jakarta-centric political ecosystem. His background as a no-nonsense businessman and a political outsider was probably one of the key motivations that drives him to demonstrate his leadership capability through a set of concrete development plans on health care, education, housing, and public infrastructure. The images of 'populist leader' and 'problem solver' – to set a contrast with other 'well-established politician' in the capital – have been projected to magnify the president's political weights.[54] Nonetheless, what is needed to sustain power is a measurable development achievement that can be seen and appreciated by the public; image projection alone is insufficient to maintain one's legitimacy in long term. In this regard, Jokowi chose to take the shortest lane possible by involving the military in various developmental projects, notably the road building and infrastructure development, and agriculture as well, among plethora of others.

Between 2014 and 2017, the TNI and the Ministry of Defence signed no less than 120 agreements with dozens of civilian ministries, universities, and social organisations.[55] From a managerial perspective, this decision seems rational, if not pragmatic. The military, thanks to its sprawling territorial structure, has personnel stationed all over the archipelago that could be deployed to assist the government to realise its agendas, and deploying the military in this regard would probably be more cost-efficient rather than contracting it out to the private sector or government-linked companies. Nonetheless, from a political perspective, the military's continued participation in civilian development plan has threatened the fabric of civil-military relations built since democratisation in 1998, especially considering that the TNI is now returning to non-defence affairs with presidential approval. It becomes logical then to assume that this invitation to return to civilian affairs has empowered the pro-status quo camp within the army to reconsolidate its internal cohesion against external criticism and to reconfigure the social identity and their political status as 'the people's army' via the advocacy of 'proxy war' and *bela negara* that in essence heavily contains, even if only implied, self-justification to be deployed in non-military sector, including but not limited to security and law enforcement, infrastructure development, public health, and education.

Taking all into account, we have demonstrated that support towards 'proxy war' and *bela negara* has been generated through multiple channels. Along with the internal push, that is, corporate interests to be involved in domestic security and other sectors and to respond to the 'global maritime fulcrum' agenda, the army has also benefited from stronger public support and the uninspiring civilian leadership, particularly under President Widodo and his over-dependence upon the officers to implement infrastructure project as well as development agenda. The complex interaction of these drivers, in return, has encouraged and provided an avenue for the army to re-contextualise its ideological principles against the external pressure to reform. The result has been worrying for the democracy; it only took a short period of time for the army to regain its assigned role as 'agent of development' in Indonesia's consolidated democracy.

Notes

1 Yong Cheol Kim, R. William Liddle, and Salim Said, "Political Leadership and Civilian Supremacy in Third Wave Democracies: Comparing South Korea and Indonesia," *Pacific Affairs* 79, 2 (2006): p. 265.

2 According to Law No. 34/2004 on TNI, the appointment of TNI commander is a prerogative right of the president. However, the law also stipulates that the president should submit the candidate to the parliament for fit and proper test. See Article 13 of Law No. 34/2004 on Indonesian National Armed Forces (Undang-undang No. 34/2004 tentang Tentara Nasional Indonesia).

3 Ristian Supriyanto, "The Superficiality of Indonesia's Defense Policy," *The Jakarta Post*, June 15, 2016, www.thejakartapost.com/academia/2016/06/15/the-superficiality-of-indonesias-defense-policy.html, accessed July 1, 2019.

4 Several points in this section are mentioned in Muhamad Haripin, "Bela Negara: Ideologi, Aparatus, dan Kritik (Defend the State: Ideology, Apparatus, and Critique)," *Jurnal Indoprogress* 1, 5 (2016): pp. 57–77.

5 Regarding the provision of *bela negara*, see Article 9 of Law No. 03/2002 on National Defence (Undang-undang No. 03/2002 tentang Pertahanan Negara).

6 Abraham Utama, "Ryamizard Targetkan 100 Juta Warga Jadi Kader Bela Negara," *CNN Indonesia*, October 12, 2015, www.cnnindonesia.com/nasional/201510121 05651-20-84362/ryamizard-targetkan-100-juta-warga-jadi-kader-bela-negara/, accessed June 15, 2017.

7 See Reza, "The Dangerous Ideology Behind Bela Negara."

8 See Haripin, "Bela Negara: Ideologi, Aparatus, dan Kritik."

9 Syaiful Hakim, "Menhan: LGBT Bagian 'Proxy War'," *Antara News*, February 23, 2013, www.antaranews.com/berita/546668/menhan-lgbt-bagian-proxy-war, accessed June 16, 2017.

10 Muhamad Haripin, "The Rise of Mass Mobilizing Politics in Indonesia," in *The Blooming Years: Kyoto Review of Southeast Asia*, ed. Pavin Chachavalpongpun (Kyoto: Center for Southeast Asian Studies – Kyoto University, 2017), pp. 611–616.

11 On the rise of FPI in Indonesian political scene and its historical context, see for instance Jajang Jahroni, *Defending the Majesty of Islam: Indonesia's Front Pembela Islam, 1998–2003* (Chiangmai: Silkworm Books, 2008).

12 The Setara Institute, a human rights advocate, urged President Joko Widodo to evaluate the implementation of *bela negara* training. Hendardi, Setara's chairman, asserted that "the immediate step for President Jokowi to take is to evaluate and ask for comprehensive accountability reports from Defence Ministry and the TNI, which run the program." See News Desk, "Jokowi Urged to Evaluate Bela Negara Following FPI Training," *The Jakarta Post*, January 9, 2017, www.thejakartapost.com/news/2017/01/09/jokowi-urged-to-evaluate-bela-negara-following-fpi-training.html, accessed June 17, 2017.

13 On the statement of military on *bela negara* and FPI, see Patricia Dyah Saraswati, "Kemhan: FPI Dilatih Berkarakter Indonesia, Bukan Islam Arab," *CNN Indonesia*, January 10, 2017, www.cnnindonesia.com/politik/20170109205650-32-185126/kemhan-fpi-dilatih-berkarakter-indonesia-bukan-islam-arab/, accessed June 15, 2017.

14 Pemuda Pancasila is a right-wing nationalist youths group – in many occasions, they also act as armed militia – established in the New Order period. The organisation used to provide strong arms for the authoritarian Suharto regime to fight and intimidate opposition camps. On the history of Pemuda Pancasila, see Loren Ryter, "Pemuda Pancasila: The Last Loyalist Free Men of Suharto's New Order?" *Indonesia* 66 (1998): pp. 45–73.

15 Saraswati, "Kemhan: FPI Dilatih Berkarakter Indonesia, Bukan Islam Arab."

16 Pancasila consists of five key principles: (1) believe in the one and only God, (2) just and civilised humanity, (3) the unity of Indonesian nation-state, (4)

democracy driven by the wisdom of deliberation, and (5) social justice for all Indonesians. On critical inquiry of *bela negara*, see Haripin, "Bela Negara: Ideologi, Aparatus, dan Kritik."

17 Margareth S. Aritonang, "State Defense Training for FPI Not Allowed: TNI," *The Jakarta Post*, January 10, 2017, www.thejakartapost.com/news/2017/01/10/state-defense-training-for-fpi-not-allowed-tni.html, accessed June 15, 2017.

18 Margareth S. Aritonang, "Defense Ministry Upholds Training for Islam Defenders Front," *The Jakarta Post*, January 11, 2017, www.thejakartapost.com/news/2017/01/11/defense-ministry-upholds-training-for-islam-defenders-front.html, accessed June 15, 2017.

19 Margareth S. Aritonang, "FPI May Join Military Training: TNI Commander," *The Jakarta Post*, January 11, 2017, www.thejakartapost.com/news/2017/01/11/fpi-may-join-military-training-tni-commander.html, accessed June 15, 2017.

20 The Lebak case was considered to be a major blow. As a military, TNI personnel should follow the procedure accordingly. In this regard, *bela negara* training in regional level must be reported hierarchically to higher level in central command. Failing to do so would cost greatly the commander. Lebak military commander Lieutenant Colonel Ubaidillah was soon replaced after the incident. See Prima Gumilang, "Kodam Siliwangi: Dandim Lebak Lakukan Kesalahan Fatal," *CNN Indonesia*, January 9, 2017, www.cnnindonesia.com/nasional/20170109112048-12-184948/kodam-siliwangi-dandim-lebak-lakukan-kesalahan-fatal/, accessed June 15, 2017.

21 For instances, Juwono supported the decision of Army General (Ret.) Wiranto, former TNI commander, to turn down the request of National Human Rights Commission (Komisi Nasional Hak Asasi Manusia: Komnas HAM) to question him regarding the allegation of involving in human rights violation in East Timor in 1999. Interview with Juwono Sudarsono in Jakarta, March 12, 2010.

22 On Yusgiantoro's view on national defence and military transformation, see Purnomo Yusgiantoro, "Pencapaian Pembangunan Pertahanan Keamanan Setelah 65 Tahun Indonesia Merdeka," *Negarawan* 17 (2010): pp. 28–53.

23 Institute for Policy Analysis of Conflict, *The Expanding Role of the Indonesian Military* (Jakarta: Institute for Policy Analysis of Conflict, 2015), pp. 14–15.

24 Karl Deutsch, "External Involvement in Internal War," in *Internal War, Problems and Approaches*, ed. Harry Eckstein (New York: Free Press of Glencoe, 1964), p. 102.

25 Early Indonesian nationalist leaders believed that major powers were competing to win Indonesia. This has made the country as merely a political commodity among the colonialists. Therefore, they argued that Indonesia should stand on its own. On the idea of national political elites on Indonesia as a 'pretty maiden,' see Franklin B. Weinstein, *Indonesia Foreign Policy and the Dilemma of Independence: From Sukarno to Soeharto* (Ithaca, NY: Cornell University Press, 1976), pp. 42–45.

26 Jun Honna made an interesting observation that by disqualifying the 1926 communist revolt against the Dutch rule as a freedom movement or liberation struggle, the New Order regime and Indonesian military are accidentally unaware to claim its position as supporter of the Dutch colonial power. See Jun Honna, "Military Ideology in Response to Democratic Pressure During the Late Suharto Era: Political and Institutional Contexts," *Indonesia* 67 (1999): p. 83.

27 On the political rivalry between the army and the communist party prior to – and that led to – the murder of army generals on September 30–October 1, 1965, in Jakarta, see Benedict Anderson, Ruth McVey, and Frederick Bunnell, *A Preliminary Analysis of the October 1, 1965 Coup in Indonesia* (Ithaca, NY and New York: Cornell University, 1971).

28 On the complex political environment of this so-called '30 September Movement' (*'Gerakan 30 September'*), see John Roosa, *Pretext for Mass Murder: The September 30th Movement and Suharto Coup D'Etat in Indonesia* (Madison: University of Wisconsin Press, 2006).

29 On a discussion about the deadly outcomes of Suharto's New Order massive and brutal anti-communist campaigns, see, for instance, Geoffrey B. Robinson, *The Killing Season: A History of the Indonesian Massacres, 1965–1966* (Princeton: Princeton University Press, 2018); Douglas Kammen and Katharine McGregor (Eds.), *The Countours of Mass Violence in Indonesia, 1965–1968* (Singapore: NUS Press, 2012); and Robert Cribb (Ed.), *The Indonesian Killings 1965–1966: Studies From Java and Bali* (Victoria: Centre for Southeast Asian Studies, Monash University, 1990).

30 On a discussion that suggests this interesting yet peculiar relation between the New Order regime and the status of 'communism' in Indonesian political discourse, see Ariel Heryanto, *State Terrorism and Political Identity in Indonesia: Fatally Belonging* (London and New York: Routledge, 2006).

31 Ichsan Emrald Alamsyah, "Jika Perang Indonesia Hanya Bertahan 3 Hari, Mengapa?" *Republika*, February 22, 2015, www.republika.co.id/berita/nasional/umum/15/02/22/nk4xxr-jika-perang-indonesia-hanya-bertahan-3-hari-mengapa, accessed May 7, 2017.

32 See, for instance, Amitav Acharya, *Indonesia Matters: Asia's Emerging Democratic Power* (Singapore: World Scientific, 2015) and Anthony Reid (Ed.), *Indonesia Rising: The Repositioning of Asia's Third Giant* (Singapore: ISEAS, 2012).

33 Edward Aspinall, "The New Nationalism in Indonesia," *Asia and the Pacific Policy Studies* 3, 1 (2016): pp. 69–79.

34 The common Indonesian translation of 'proxy war' is *'perang proksi.'*

35 Keoni Marzuki, "Proxy Wars Narrative: TNI-AD's Quest for Relevance?" *RSIS Commentaries*, April 21, 2016, p. 1.

36 Azyumardi Azra, "Proxy War (2)," *Republika*, August 20, 2015, www.republika.co.id/berita/kolom/resonansi/15/08/19/ntbxsu319-proxy-war-2, accessed May 29, 2017.

37 Azyumardi Azra, "Proxy War (1)," *Republika*, August 13, 2015, www.republika.co.id/berita/kolom/resonansi/15/08/12/nsz4pi319-proxy-war-1, accessed May 29, 2017.

38 Dylan Aprialdo Rachman, "TNI Diminta Fokus Hadapi Ancaman 'Proxy War'," *Kompas*, October 5, 2015, http://nasional.kompas.com/read/2015/10/05/16355011/TNI.Diminta.Fokus.Hadapi.Ancaman.Proxy.War, accessed May 30, 2017.

39 Dani Prabowo, "Empat Tantangan Besar bagi TNI pada Usia ke-70," *Kompas*, October 5, 2015, http://nasional.kompas.com/read/2015/10/05/11490191/Empat.Tantangan.Besar.bagi.TNI.pada.Usia.Ke-70, accessed May 30, 2017.

40 Nabilla Tashandra, "Uji Kelayakan Calon Panglima TNI, Hadi Paparkan Terorisme hingga Perang Siber," *Kompas*, December 6, 2017, https://nasional.kompas.com/read/2017/12/06/12391091/uji-kelayakan-calon-panglima-tni-hadi-paparkan-terorisme-hingga-perang-siber, accessed July 3, 2019.

41 Fabian Kuwado, "Panglima TNI Instruksikan Komandan Satuan Waspadai Perang Asimetris," *Kompas*, January 26, 2018, https://nasional.kompas.com/read/2018/01/26/10463391/panglima-tni-instruksikan-komandan-satuan-waspadai-perang-asimetris, accessed July 3, 2019.

42 On Yudhoyono presidency and his score points throughout a decade in office, see the interesting edited volume of Edward Aspinall, Marcus Mietzner, and

Dirk Tomsa (Eds.), *The Yudhoyono Presidency: Indonesia's Decade of Stability and Stagnation* (Singapore: ISEAS, 2015).

43 Institute for Policy Analysis of Conflict, *The Expanding Role of the Indonesian Military*, p. 14.

44 On the roles and function of the Indonesian National Police (Kepolisian Negara Republik Indonesia: Polri), see Articles 13, 14, 15, and 16 of Law No. 02/2002 on Indonesian National Police (Undang-undang No. 02/2002 tentang Kepolisian Negara Republik Indonesia).

45 See, for example, Taufiq Siddiq, "Survei Charta Politika: TNI Lembaga Paling Dipercaya Publik," *Tempo*, August 28, 2018, https://nasional.tempo.co/read/1121454/survei-charta-politika-tni-lembaga-paling-dipercaya-publik/full& view=ok, accessed July 3, 2019, and Ambaranie Movanita, "Survei Kompas: Citra TNI hingga 94 Persen, Citra DPR Terendah," *Kompas*, October 21, 2017, https://nasional.kompas.com/read/2017/10/21/07122651/survei-kompas-citra-tni-naik-hingga-94-persen-citra-dpr-terendah, accessed July 3, 2019.

46 See Rizal Sukma, "The Military and Democratic Reform in Indonesia," in *Military Engagement: Influencing Armed Forces Worldwide to Support Democratic Transitions*, ed. Dennis Blair (Washington, DC: Brookings Institution Press, 2013), p. 123 and Muhammad Najib Azca, "Security Sector Reform, Democratic Transition and Social Violence: The Case of Ambon, Indonesia," in *Security Sector Reform: Potentials and Challenges for Conflict Transformation*, eds. Clem McCartney, Martina Fischer, and Olver Wils (Berlin: Berghof Research Center for Constructive Conflict Management, 2004).

47 Marzuki, "Proxy Wars Narrative," p. 3.

48 Rendi A. Witular, "Jokowi Launches Maritime Doctrine to the World," *The Jakarta Post*, November 13, 2014, www.thejakartapost.com/news/2014/11/13/jokowi-launches-maritime-doctrine-world.html, accessed June 11, 2017.

49 Aaron L. Connelly, "The Sovereignty and the Sea: Joko Widodo's Foreign Policy Challenges," *Contemporary Southeast Asia* 37, 1 (2015): p. 18.

50 Asia Sentinel, "Jokowi's Tough New Maritime Policy Takes Shape," *Asia Sentinel*, December 9, 2014, www.asiasentinel.com/econ-business/jokowi-tough-new-maritime-policy-takes-shape/, accessed June 12, 2017.

51 Interview with Lieutenant General (Ret.) Agus Widjojo in Jakarta, September 6, 2016.

52 Institute for Policy Analysis of Conflict, *The Expanding Role of the Indonesian Military*, p. 13.

53 Interview of Institute for Policy Analysis of Conflict (IPAC) with TNI officer in Jakarta, December 10, 2015. See Institute for Policy Analysis of Conflict, *Update on the Indonesian Military's Influence*, p. 2.

54 On Jokowi's populism, see Marcus Mietzner, *Reinventing Asian Populism: Jokowi's Rise, Democracy, and Political Contestation in Indonesia* (Honolulu: East-West Center, 2015).

55 Evan A. Laksmana, "Reshuffling the Deck? Military Corporatism, Promotional Logjams and Post-Authoritarian Civil-Military Relations in Indonesia," *Journal of Contemporary Asia* 49, 5 (2019): p. 807.

5 Conclusion

Ideology and democratic setback

*Muhamad Haripin, Adhi Priamarizki,
and Keoni Indrabayu Marzuki*

We have discussed the ideological journey of Indonesian army in the span of seven decades. What can be learned from such a long history? How will it inform us about the ideology, civil-military relations, and democratisation in Indonesia in the years to come?

Here, obviously political and historical continuities are apparent in many instances. Ideology, a set of certain beliefs pertaining to strategic outlook, has been continuously exploited to invigorate the army's political stance against potential and imminent threats. Indeed, what is considered threats has always been at the core of political contestation. We have shown that the introduction or reinvention of ideology comes as a result of the dynamics within the internal military organisation searching for meaning in politics and to actualise its political aspiration. In another occasion, the army elites have exploited the military's ideology as a means to justify its own stance against the opposition and general public.

The military during the New Order period had strategically cemented dual-functions at the core of its doctrinal structure and forcefully immersed it as an undisputable political norm. Nonetheless, our discussion on the army ideology during Sukarno and Suharto years must be understood in its own historical context, meaning it emerged during the tumultuous period of post-colonialism and then followed by the authoritarian era, which implies that military intervention can be regarded to be a 'logical' path of action – due to the complex situation that has been illustrated in the previous section. Such 'state of emergency' or 'exception' could also be applied to explain the proliferation of army ideology in the democratic transition period. The country was shaken by simultaneous economic and political crisis, which then was followed by several other crises such as social conflict, separatism, and terrorist attacks. The military had a strong case – though not necessarily justifiable – to advance its position and to retain past privileges in order to protect the country from the brink of disintegration. These were years of living dangerously for the average Indonesians, so to speak.

Nevertheless, the current 'proxy war' and *bela negara* ideology, on the contrary, shows us a rather peculiar development. No form of existential threat has been threatening the Indonesian nation-state in recent years, especially during Susilo Bambang Yudhoyono and Joko Widodo administrations, since the Indonesian government agreed to end hostilities with Free Aceh Movement (Gerakan Aceh Merdeka: GAM) in August 2005. Indeed, terrorist attacks and social conflicts continue to be major security issues for the country, but they hardly ever escalate uncontrollably and endanger the fabric of society. In political sector, some encouraging developments are evident, for example, the peaceful transfer of power, a continuing free press, and the emergence of accomplished local leaders. Therefore, it might be fair to assume that the country has entered the democratic consolidation period.

This phase, we argue, is the tipping point of Indonesian army ideology. Rather than acting in a typical defensive way, the army propagates the ideologies of 'proxy war' and 'defend the state' to broaden their current prevailing political power. This expansionist nature is the new feature of Indonesian army ideology. By exploiting the politics of fear, that is, that the country is under attack from all direction, perpetrated by state as well as non-state actors, the army establishment and its counterpart in the Ministry of Defence devised a sophisticated justification in order to have more say and flexible jurisdiction in non-military affairs.

Why does the military take this action? Through previous discussion, we suggest that the military's attempt to reinvigorate its institutional interests, including prestige, against other branches of the armed forces, that is, navy and air force, is a response to the new agenda of 'global maritime fulcrum,' advocated by current civilian President Widodo. In other words, the military simply seeks to reinforce its political status and organisational capability in an aspiring maritime-oriented Indonesia.

Interestingly, the introduction of 'proxy war' and *bela negara* was not followed by re-envisioning the *Paradigma Baru*, or development of a new military doctrine that encapsulates the foundational ideas of both 'proxy war' and *bela negara*. This situation contradicts what previous studies have concluded regarding the central role of doctrine in facilitating military political intervention. This study has shown that the TNI is still able, to some extent, to preserve its interventionist behaviour without significantly altering the military doctrine. We can also conclude that 'proxy war' and *bela negara* have become instruments of the military to safeguard its corporate interests, without completely resisting the idea of reform.

As shown by case studies in other countries, the civilian leadership partly contributed to military's meddling in politics. On top of that, it is the civilian authority who oftentimes invites the military to take part in governance or join his or her political struggle against opposition groups.

Indonesia's Joko Widodo is not an exception. Moreover, given its vast territorial command network and personnel size across the archipelago, it would
be hard to undermine the military potential contribution from any serious
effort to develop the country's lagging infrastructure. *Dwifungsi* was precisely implemented to support the government in implementing New Order
developmentalist agenda. The current President Joko Widodo has apparently found the value of the military to help him build necessary system,
organisation, and network required to boost the national economy. Against
this backdrop, Jokowi's early years of presidency have demonstrated that a
weak and dependent civilian leadership plays some roles in contemporary
civil-military relations in Indonesia.

Taking all this into account, this study has demonstrated the intricate
relationship of the TNI's recurring ideological manoeuvres and military
politics in the democratic consolidation period. In contrast with the existing literatures that tend to overlook the role of ideology in shaping military
behaviour, we have explained that the proliferation of 'proxy war' and *bela
negara* ideologies is a key point to fathom the latest expression of TNI's
expansionist gestures upon the current Indonesian polity. In this regard, the
meticulous analysis and findings drawn from political and historical perspective in preceding chapters should be underlined as the main contribu-
tions of this study to the scholarship of Indonesian studies and civil-military
relations studies.

Furthermore, the arrival of democratisation that forced the military to
come up with a new ideology which fits with democratic environment provided no assurance to prevent the formulation of an interventionist thinking.
The case of Indonesia displayed political reform had forced the military to
formulate an ideology that suits the democratic environment following the
end of the New Order regime. While such an ideology persists, the Indonesian army found another way around to defend its corporate interests via
creation of ancillary thinking that are 'proxy war' and *bela negara*. As a
result, the military can deceive the democratic demand and reform pressure
through formulation of parasitic as well as interventionist thinking without
officially altering the existing military ideology.

References

Acharya, Amitav. *Indonesia Matters: Asia's Emerging Democratic Power* (Singapore: World Scientific, 2015).

Adams, Cindy. *Soekarno: An Autobiography, as Told to Cindy Adams* (Indianapolis, Kansas City, and New York: The Bobbs-Merrill Company Inc., 1965).

Alagappa, Muthiah. "Comprehensive Security: Interpretations in ASEAN Countries." In *Asian Security Issues: Regional and Global*, eds. Robert A. Scalapino, et al. (Berkeley: Institute of East Asian Studies of the University of California, 1982), pp. 50–78.

Alagappa, Muthiah. "Investigating and Explaining Change: An Analytical Framework." In *Coercion and Governance: The Declining Political Role of the Military in Asia*, ed. Muthiah Alagappa (Stanford: Stanford University Press, 2001), pp. 29–68.

Anderson, Benedict, Ruth McVey, and Frederick Bunnell. *A Preliminary Analysis of the October 1, 1965 Coup in Indonesia* (Ithaca and New York: Cornell University, 1971).

Anwar, Dewi Fortuna. "Indonesia: *Ketahanan Nasional, Wawasan Nusantara, Hankamrata*." In *Strategic Cultures in the Asia-Pacific Region*, eds. Ken Booth and Russell Trood (New York: St. Martin's Press, 1999), pp. 199–224.

Aspinall, Edward. "The New Nationalism in Indonesia." *Asia and the Pacific Policy Studies* 3, 1 (2016): pp. 69–79.

Aspinall, Edward, Marcus Mietzner, and Dirk Tomsa (Eds.). *The Yudhoyono Presidency: Indonesia's Decade of Stability and Stagnation* (Singapore: ISEAS, 2015).

Azca, Muhammad Najib. "Security Sector Reform, Democratic Transition and Social Violence: The Case of Ambon, Indonesia." In *Security Sector Reform: Potentials and Challenges for Conflict Transformation*, eds. Clem McCartney, Martina Fischer, and Oliver Wils (Berlin: Berghof Research Center for Constructive Conflict Management, 2004), pp. 35–44.

Baker, Nicola and Leonard C. Sebastian. "The Problem With Parachuting: Strategic Studies and Security in the Asia/Pacific Region." *The Journal of Strategic Studies* 18, 3 (1995): pp. 15–31.

Ball, Desmond. "Strategic Culture in the Asia-Pacific Region." *Security Studies* 3, 1 (1993): pp. 44–74.

Barany, Zoltan. *The Soldier and the Changing State: Building Democratic Armies in Africa, Asia, Europe, and the Americas* (Princeton and Oxford: Princeton University Press, 2012).

Bourchier, David. *Illiberal Democracy in Indonesia: The Ideology of the Family State* (New York: Routledge, 2015).

Bradford, John. "The Indonesian Military as a Professional Organization: Criteria and Ramifications for Reform." *RSIS Working Paper* No. 73 (2005).

Britton, Peter A. *Profesionalisme dan Ideologi Militer Indonesia: Perspektif Tradisi-Tradisi Jawa dan Barat* (Jakarta: LP3ES, 1996).

Connelly, Aaron L. "The Sovereignty and the Sea: Joko Widodo's Foreign Policy Challenges." *Contemporary Southeast Asia* 37, 1 (2015): pp. 1–28.

Cribb, Robert (Ed.). *The Indonesian Killings 1965–1966: Studies From Java and Bali* (Victoria: Centre for Southeast Asian Studies, Monash University, 1990).

Croissant, Aurel. *Civil-Military Relations in Southeast Asia* (Cambridge: Cambridge University Press, 2018).

Crouch, Harold. *The Army and Politics in Indonesia* (Ithaca, NY: Cornell University Press, 1978).

Crouch, Harold. *Political Reform in Indonesia After Soeharto* (Singapore: ISEAS, 2010).

Daves, Joseph H. *The Indonesian Army From Revolusi to Reformasi – Volume 1: The Struggle for Independence and the Sukarno Era* (CreateSpace Independent Publishing Platform, 2013).

Deutsch, Karl. "External Involvement in Internal War." In *Internal War, Problems and Approaches*, ed. Harry Eckstein (New York: Free Press of Glencoe, 1964), pp. 100–110.

Duncan, Christopher R. *Violence and Vengeance: Religious Conflict and Its Aftermath in Eastern Indonesia* (Ithaca, NY: Cornell University Press, 2013).

Egreteau, Renaud and Larry Jagan. *Soldiers and Diplomacy in Burma: Understanding the Foreign Relations of the Burmese Praetorian State* (Singapore: NUS Press, 2013).

Emmers, Ralf. "Comprehensive Security and Resilience in Southeast Asia: ASEAN's Approach to Terrorism." *The Pacific Review* 22, 2 (2009): pp. 159–177.

Finer, Samuel. *The Man on Horseback: The Role of the Military in Politics* (4th printing) (New Brunswick and London: Transaction Publishers, 2006).

Haripin, Muhamad. "Bela Negara: Ideologi, Aparatus, dan Kritik (Defend the State: Ideology, Apparatus, and Critique)." *Jurnal Indoprogress* 1, 5 (2016): pp. 57–77.

Haripin, Muhamad. *Civil–Military Relations in Indonesia: The Politics of Military Operations Other Than War* (London: Routledge, 2019).

Haripin, Muhamad. "The Rise of Mass Mobilizing Politics in Indonesia." In *The Blooming Years: Kyoto Review of Southeast Asia*, ed. Pavin Chachavalpongpun (Kyoto: Center for Southeast Asian Studies – Kyoto University, 2017), pp. 611–616.

Hefner, Robert. *Civil Islam: Muslims and Democratization in Indonesia* (Princeton: Princeton University Press, 2000).

Heryanto, Ariel. *State Terrorism and Political Identity in Indonesia: Fatally Belonging* (London and New York: Routledge, 2006).

Honna, Jun. "From Dwifungsi to NKRI. Regime Change and Political Activism of the Indonesian Military." In *Democratization in Post-Suharto Indonesia*, eds. Marco Bünte and Andreas Ufen (London and New York: Routledge, 2009), pp. 226–248.

Honna, Jun. "Military Ideology in Response to Democratic Pressure During the Late Suharto Era: Political and Institutional Contexts." *Indonesia* 67 (1999): pp. 77–126.

Honna, Jun. *Military Politics and Democratization in Indonesia* (London: Routledge, 2003).

Honna, Jun. "Security Challenges and Military Reform in Post-authoritarian Indonesia: The Impact of Separatism, Terrorism, and Communal Violence." In *The Politics of Military Reform: Experiences From Indonesia and Nigeria*, eds. Jürgen Rüland, Maria-Gabriela Manea, and Hans Born (Heidelberg: Springer, 2013), pp. 185–201.

Huntington, Samuel. *The Third Wave: Democratization in the Late Twentieth Century* (Norman: University of Oklahoma Press, 1991).

Institute for Policy Analysis of Conflict. *The Expanding Role of the Indonesian Military* (Jakarta: Institute for Policy Analysis of Conflict, 2015).

Institute for Policy Analysis of Conflict. *Update on the Indonesian Military's Influence* (Jakarta: Institute for Policy Analysis of Conflict, 2016).

Jahroni, Jajang. *Defending the Majesty of Islam: Indonesia's Front Pembela Islam, 1998–2003* (Chiangmai: Silkworm Books, 2008).

Janowitz, Moris. *Military Institutions and Coercion in the Developing Nations* (Chicago and London: The University of Chicago Press, 1977).

Jenkins, David. *Soeharto and His Generals: Indonesian Military Politics 1975–1983* (3rd Edition) (New York, NY: Cornell University, 1997).

Joes, Anthony J. *Resisting Rebellion: The History and Politics of Counterinsurgency* (Lexington: The University Press of Kentucky, 2004).

Kammen, Douglas and Katharine McGregor (Eds.). *The Contours of Mass Violence in Indonesia, 1965–1968* (Singapore: NUS Press, 2012).

Kim, Yong Cheol, R. William Liddle, and Salim Said. "Political Leadership and Civilian Supremacy in Third Wave Democracies: Comparing South Korea and Indonesia." *Pacific Affairs* 79, 2 (2006): pp. 247–268.

Kingsbury, Damien. *Power Politics and the Indonesian Military* (New York: RoutledgeCurzon, 2003).

Koonings, Kees and Dirk Kruijt. "Epilogue: Political Armies Between Continuity and Demise." In *Political Armies: The Military and Nation Building in the Age of Democracy*, eds. Kees Koonings and Dirk Kruijt (New York: Zed Books, 2002), pp. 333–347.

Kusumaatmadja, Mochtar. "Some Thoughts on ASEAN Security Co-operation: An Indonesian Perspective." *Contemporary Southeast Asia* 12, 3 (1990): pp. 161–171.

Laksmana, Evan A. "Indonesia's Modernizing Military: Suharto's New Order Is Old News." *Foreign Affairs*, September 3, 2015.

Laksmana, Evan A. "Rebalancing Indonesia's Naval Force: Trends, Nature and Drivers." In *Naval Modernisation in South-East Asia: Nature, Causes and*

Consequences, eds. Geoffrey Till and Jane Chan (London: Routledge, 2014), pp. 175–203.

Laksmana, Evan A. "Reshuffling the Deck? Military Corporatism, Promotional Logjams and Post-Authoritarian Civil-Military Relations in Indonesia." *Journal of Contemporary Asia* 49, 5 (2019): pp. 806–836.

Laksmana, Evan A. "The Enduring Strategic Trinity: Explaining Indonesia's Geopolitical Architecture." *Journal of the Indian Ocean Region* 7, 1 (2011): pp. 95–116.

Law No. 02/2002 on Indonesian National Police (Undang-undang No. 02/2002 tentang Kepolisian Negara Republik Indonesia).

Law No. 03/2002 on National Defence (Undang-undang No. 03/2002 tentang Pertahanan Negara).

Law No. 34/2004 on Indonesian National Armed Forces (Undang-undang No. 34/2004 tentang Tentara Nasional Indonesia).

Marzuki, Keoni. "Proxy Wars Narrative: TNI-AD's Quest for Relevance?" *RSIS Commentaries*, April 21, 2016.

McCulloch, Lesley. "*Trifungsi:* The Role of the Indonesian Military in Business." In *The Military as an Economic Actor: Soldiers in Business*, eds. Jörn Brömmelhörster and Wolf-Christian Paes (New York: Palgrave Macmillan, 2003), pp. 94–124.

McGregor, Katharine. *History in Uniform: Military Ideology and the Construction of Indonesia's Past* (Singapore: National University of Singapore Press, 2007).

McRae, Dave. *A Few Poorly Organized Men: Interreligious Violence in Poso, Indonesia* (Leiden: Brill, 2013).

McVey, Ruth T. "The Post Revolutionary Transformation of the Indonesia Army." *Indonesia* 11 (1971): pp. 131–176.

McVey, Ruth T. "The Post-Revolutionary Transformation of the Indonesian Army Part II." *Indonesia* 13 (1972): pp. 147–181.

Mietzner, Marcus. *Military Politics, Islam, and the State in Indonesia: From Turbulent Transition to Democratic Consolidation* (Singapore: ISEAS, 2009).

Mietzner, Marcus. "The Political Marginalization of the Military in Indonesia." In *The Political Resurgence of the Military in Southeast Asia*, ed. Marcus Mietzner (London and New York: Routledge, 2011), pp. 216–247.

Mietzner, Marcus. *Reinventing Asian Populism: Jokowi's Rise, Democracy, and Political Contestation in Indonesia* (Honolulu: East-West Center, 2015).

Muradi. *Politics and Governance in Indonesia: The Police in the Era of Reformasi* (New York: Routledge, 2014).

Nordlinger, Eric A. *Soldiers in Politics: Military Coups and Governments* (Englewood Cliffs, NJ: Prentice-Hall, 1977).

Perlmutter, Amos. *The Military and Politics in Modern Times* (New Haven and London: Yale University Press, 1977).

Perlmutter, Amos. "The Praetorian State and the Praetorian Army: Towards a Taxonomy of Civil-Military Relations in Developing Countries." *Comparative Politics* 1, 3 (1969): pp. 382–404.

Prasetyo, Stanley Adi and Toriq Hadad. *Jenderal Tanpa Pasukan, Politisi Tanpa Partai: Perjalanan Hidup A. H. Nasution* (Jakarta: Pusat Data dan Analisa Tempo dan Institut Studi Arus Informasi, 2007).

Reid, Anthony (Ed.). *Indonesia Rising: The Repositioning of Asia's Third Giant* (Singapore: ISEAS, 2012).

Rieffel, Lex and Jaleswari Pramodhawardani. *Out of Business and On Budget: The Challenge of Military Financing in Indonesia* (Washington, DC: The Brookings Institution, 2007).

Rinakit, Sukardi. *The Indonesian Military After the New Order* (Denmark and Singapore: NIAS Press and ISEAS, 2005).

Robinson, Geoffrey B. *The Killing Season: A History of the Indonesian Massacres, 1965–1966* (Princeton: Princeton University Press, 2018).

Rocher, Jean and Iwan Santosa. *KNIL* (Jakarta: Kompas, 2016).

Roosa, John. *Pretext for Mass Murder: The September 30th Movement and Suharto Coup D'Etat in Indonesia* (Madison: University of Wisconsin Press, 2006).

Ryter, Loren. "Pemuda Pancasila: The Last Loyalist Free Men of Suharto's New Order?" *Indonesia* 66 (1998): pp. 45–73.

Said, Salim. *Genesis of Power: General Sudirman and the Indonesia Military in Politics, 1945–49* (Singapore: ISEAS, 1992).

Said, Salim. "The Political Role of the Indonesian Military: Past, Present and Future." *Asian Journal of Social Science* 15, 1 (1987): pp. 16–34.

Sebastian, Leonard C. *Realpolitik Ideology: Indonesia's Use of Military Force* (Singapore: ISEAS, 2006).

Sebastian, Leonard C. and Iis Gindarsah. "Taking Stock of Military Reform in Indonesia." In *The Politics of Military Reform: Experiences From Indonesia and Nigeria*, eds. Jürgen Rüland, Maria-Gabriela Manea, and Hans Born (Heidelberg: Springer, 2013), pp. 29–57.

Shah, Aqil. *The Army and Democracy: Military Politics in Pakistan* (Cambridge, MA: Harvard University Press, 2014).

Sidel, John T. *Riots, Pogroms, Jihad: Religious Violence in Indonesia* (Ithaca, NY and London: Cornell University Press, 2006).

Stepan, Alfred. *The Military in Politics: Changing Patterns in Brazil* (Princeton: Princeton University Press, 1971).

Stepan, Alfred. "The New Professionalism of Internal Warfare and Military Role Expansion." In *Authoritarian Brazil: Origins, Policies, and Future*, ed. Alfred Stepan (London: Yale University Press, 1976), pp 47–65.

Sukma, Rizal. "The Military and Democratic Reform in Indonesia." In *Military Engagement: Influencing Armed Forces Worldwide to Support Democratic Transitions*, ed. Dennis Blair (Washington, DC: Brookings Institution Press, 2013), pp. 113–138.

Sumbogo, Priyono B. "Jalan Tengah dan Dwifungsi." *GATRA*, March 8, 1997.

Sundhaussen, Ulf. *The Road to Power: Indonesian Military Politics, 1945–1967* (Kuala Lumpur: Oxford University Press, 1982).

Suryadinata, Leo. "The Decline of the Hegemonic Party System in Indonesia: Golkar After the Fall of Soeharto." *Contemporary Southeast Asia* 29, 2 (2007): pp. 333–358.

Tajima, Yuhki. *The Institutional Origins of Communal Violence: Indonesia's Transition From Authoritarian Rule* (New York: Cambridge University Press, 2014).

van Klinken, Gerry. *Communal Violence and Democratization in Indonesia: Small Town Wars* (London and New York: Routledge, 2007).

Weinstein, Franklin B. *Indonesia Foreign Policy and the Dilemma of Independence: From Sukarno to Soeharto* (Ithaca, NY: Cornell University Press, 1976).

Widoyoko, Danang, et al. *Bisnis Militer Mencari Legitimasi* (Jakarta: ICW, 2003).

Yusgiantoro, Purnomo. "Pencapaian Pembangunan Pertahanan Keamanan Setelah 65 Tahun Indonesia Merdeka." *Negarawan* 17 (2010): pp. 28–53.

Online sources

Alamsyah, Ichsan Emrald. "Jika Perang Indonesia Hanya Bertahan 3 Hari, Mengapa?" *Republika*, February 22, 2015, www.republika.co.id/berita/nasional/umum/15/02/22/nk4xxr-jika-perang-indonesia-hanya-bertahan-3-hari-mengapa, accessed May 7, 2017.

Aritonang, Margareth S. "Defense Ministry Upholds Training for Islam Defenders Front." *The Jakarta Post*, January 11, 2017, www.thejakartapost.com/news/2017/01/11/defense-ministry-upholds-training-for-islam-defenders-front.html, accessed June 15, 2017.

Aritonang, Margareth S. "FPI May Join Military Training: TNI Commander." *The Jakarta Post*, January 11, 2017, www.thejakartapost.com/news/2017/01/11/fpi-may-join-military-training-tni-commander.html, accessed June 15, 2017.

Aritonang, Margareth S. "State Defense Training for FPI Not Allowed: TNI." *The Jakarta Post*, January 10, 2017, www.thejakartapost.com/news/2017/01/10/state-defense-training-for-fpi-not-allowed-tni.html, accessed June 15, 2017.

Asia Sentinel. "Jokowi's Tough New Maritime Policy Takes Shape." *Asia Sentinel*, December 9, 2014, www.asiasentinel.com/econ-business/jokowi-tough-new-maritime-policy-takes-shape/, accessed June 12, 2017.

Azra, Azyumardi. "Proxy War (1)." *Republika*, August 13, 2015, www.republika.co.id/berita/kolom/resonansi/15/08/12/nsz4pi319-proxy-war-1, accessed May 29, 2017.

Azra, Azyumardi. "Proxy War (2)." *Republika*, August 20, 2015, www.republika.co.id/berita/kolom/resonansi/15/08/19/ntbxsu319-proxy-war-2, accessed May 29, 2017.

Evie, A. D. "Danlantamal II Adakan Komsos TNI Matra Laut TA 2018 di TPI Muara Angke." *Radio Republik Indonesia*, March 30, 2018, http://rri.co.id/post/berita/508537/press_release/danlantamal_iii_adakan_komsos_tni_matra_laut_ta_2018_di_tpi_muara_angke.html, accessed June 28, 2019.

Gumilang, Prima. "Kodam Siliwangi: Dandim Lebak Lakukan Kesalahan Fatal." *CNN Indonesia*, January 9, 2017, www.cnnindonesia.com/nasional/20170109112048-12-184948/kodam-siliwangi-dandim-lebak-lakukan-kesalahan-fatal/, accessed June 15, 2017.

Hakim, Syaiful. "Menhan: LGBT Bagian 'Proxy War'." *Antara News*, February 23, 2013, www.antaranews.com/berita/546668/menhan-lgbt-bagian-proxy-war, accessed June 16, 2017.

The Jakarta Post News Desk. "Jokowi Urged to Evaluate Bela Negara Following FPI Training." *The Jakarta Post*, January 9, 2017, www.thejakartapost.com/news/2017/01/09/jokowi-urged-to-evaluate-bela-negara-following-fpi-training.html, accessed June 17, 2017.

Kuwado, Fabian. "Panglima TNI Instruksikan Komandan Satuan Waspadai Perang Asimetris." *Kompas*, January 26, 2018, https://nasional.kompas.com/read/2018/01/26/10463391/panglima-tni-instruksikan-komandan-satuan-waspadai-perang-asimetris, accessed July 3, 2019.

Moenanto, Gede. "Wawasan Kebangsaan dan Bela Negara di Tengah Arus Proxy War." *Tribun News*, May 30, 2016, www.tribunnews.com/metropolitan/2016/05/30/wawasan-kebangsaan-dan-bela-negara-di-tengah-arus-proxy-war, accessed June 28, 2019.

Movanita, Ambaranie. "Survei Kompas: Citra TNI hingga 94 Persen, Citra DPR Terendah." *Kompas*, October 21, 2017, https://nasional.kompas.com/read/2017/10/21/07122651/survei-kompas-citra-tni-naik-hingga-94-persen-citra-dpr-terendah, accessed July 3, 2019.

Prabowo, Dani. "Empat Tantangan Besar bagi TNI pada Usia ke-70." *Kompas*, October 5, 2015, http://nasional.kompas.com/read/2015/10/05/11490191/Empat. Tantangan.Besar.bagi.TNI.pada.Usia.Ke-70, accessed May 30, 2017.

Rachman, Dylan Aprialdo. "TNI Diminta Fokus Hadapi Ancaman 'Proxy War.'" *Kompas*, October 5, 2015, http://nasional.kompas.com/read/2015/10/05/16355011/TNI. Diminta.Fokus.Hadapi.Ancaman.Proxy.War, accessed May 30, 2017.

Reza, Bhatara Ibnu. "Bela Negara: Thinly Veiled Militarisation of the Civilian Population." *Indonesia at Melbourne*, July 12, 2016, http://indonesiaatmelbourne. unimelb.edu.au/bela-negara-thinly-veiled-militarisation-of-the-civilian-population/, accessed May 16, 2017.

Reza, Bhatara Ibnu. "The Dangerous Ideology Behind Bela Negara." *New Mandala*, January 25, 2017, www.newmandala.org/dangerous-ideology-behind-bela-negara/, accessed May 16, 2017.

Saraswati, Patricia Dyah. "Kemhan: FPI Dilatih Berkarakter Indonesia, Bukan Islam Arab." *CNN Indonesia*, January 10, 2017, www.cnnindonesia.com/politik/20170109205650-32-185126/kemhan-fpi-dilatih-berkarakter-indonesia-bukan-islam-arab/, accessed June 15, 2017.

Sardjana, I Gede Wajan. *Civil–Military Relations: The Role of ABRI in Indonesian Socio-Political Life* (Master Thesis) (Monterey: Naval Post Graduate School, 1995), http://calhoun.nps.edu/bitstream/handle/10945/31485/95Jun_Sardjana.pdf?sequence=1&isAllowed=y, accessed August 5, 2017.

Siddiq, Taufiq. "Survei Charta Politika: TNI Lembaga Paling Dipercaya Publik." *Tempo*, August 28, 2018, https://nasional.tempo.co/read/1121454/survei-charta-politika-tni-lembaga-paling-dipercaya-publik/full&view=ok, accessed July 3, 2019.

Supriyanto, Ristian. "The Superficiality of Indonesia's Defense Policy." *The Jakarta Post*, June 15, 2016, www.thejakartapost.com/academia/2016/06/15/the-superficiality-of-indonesias-defense-policy.html, accessed July 1, 2019.

Tashandra, Nabilla. "Uji Kelayakan Calon Panglima TNI, Hadi Paparkan Terorisme hingga Perang Siber." *Kompas*, December 6, 2017, https://nasional.kompas.com/read/2017/12/06/12391091/uji-kelayakan-calon-panglima-tni-hadi-paparkan-terorisme-hingga-perang-siber, accessed July 3, 2019.

Tentara Nasional Indonesia Angkatan Udara. "Mewaspadai Proxy War, Lanud Iswahjudi Adakan Komsos TNI." September 15, 2017, https://tni-au.mil.id/mewaspadai-proxy-war-lanud-iwj-adakan-komsos-tni-2/, accessed June 28, 2019.

Utama, Abraham. "Ryamizard Targetkan 100 Juta Warga Jadi Kader Bela Negara." *CNN Indonesia*, October 12, 2015, www.cnnindonesia.com/nasional/20151012105651-20-84362/ryamizard-targetkan-100-juta-warga-jadi-kader-bela-negara/, accessed June 15, 2017.

Witular, Rendi A. "Jokowi Launches Maritime Doctrine to the World." *The Jakarta Post*, November 13, 2014, www.thejakartapost.com/news/2014/11/13/jokowi-launches-maritime-doctrine-world.html, accessed June 11, 2017.

Index

Note: Page numbers in *italics* indicate figures, and those in **bold** indicate tables

For Product Safety Concerns and Information please contact our EU
representative GPSR@taylorandfrancis.com
Taylor & Francis Verlag GmbH, Kaufingerstraße 24, 80331 München, Germany